Hunger Driven

By Brian Nickens
briannickens.com

This is my journey of personal
Spiritual reformation into the
supernatural Christian lifestyle.

Cover design by Jonny Giddens
cornishphotographer.com

Edited by Anna Elkins
annaelkins.com

Hunger Driven
Brian Nickens Copyright © 2015 Brian Nickens

Dedication

I dedicate this book to my dear friend Gary Wenzel. In February of 2014 Gary became absent from his body thus present with the Lord. Gary was one of the most Hunger Driven individuals I ever knew. He would fly anywhere, drive any distance and pay any price to encounter God. And this we did together many times. I miss our road trips, worship times, bible studies, intense debates and crazy adventures. I look forward to seeing him again one day. I also extend my love and prayers to April Wenzel and Scott Vanbuskirk. Thanks for your friendship and kindness.

Comments from friends

Eric Johnson
Senior Leader - Bethel Church in Redding, CA
Author of Christ In You

Almost every time I have a chat with Brian Nickens we find ourselves chatting about what God is doing or about some amazing miracle that took place recently. I am always encouraged and moved! In this book *Hunger Driven*, Brian takes us on a journey to live a life that is teeming with hope for the impossible, to see the Kingdom of Light advance and ultimately to make God known to all. Enjoy!

Brian "Head" Welch
New York Times Best Selling Author of
Save Me From Myself
KoRn

I've had the privilege of ministering with Brian and got to witness his raw, fearless faith change the atmosphere on a stage with hundreds of people and later that night in a Denny's restaurant. Brian definitely helped light a fire in me to hunger for a new and exciting faith in our supernatural God to move through me like never before.

Kevin Dedmon Author of
The Ultimate Treasure Hunt
Unlocking Heaven
The Risk Factor.
B.A. Biblical Studies
M.A. Leadership Development
Vanguard University.

Brian Nickens did not just write a book called, Hunger Driven — He is hunger driven. I have known Brian for several years as a personal friend, and I can assure you that you will get equipped, empowered and activated to take risk to enter into the supernatural Kingdom lifestyle that Brian has made normal. Brian is a world changer, and I believe that in reading his book, you will receive an impartation to change the world around you one encounter at a time. The world is waiting for a presentation and a demonstration of the Good News of great joy through signs and wonders, miracles, healing, and the prophetic. This book will help you to release God's presence and power wherever you go, to whomever you meet.

Table Of Contents

Foreword

If you have ever said to yourself "there must be more" to following Christ? Then this book is for you. If you've ever had an unexplainable hunger for God, and have sensed that there is a realm in God that appears out of reach? Then this book is for you. Brian and Doreen's story will open your eyes to the possibilities that God made available to every believer. I expect this book to both inspire and give insight as Brian boldly declares the God-process that completely changed his approach to life, making him a believing believer with profound impact on his surroundings. *Hunger Driven* will encourage you to say yes to God's invitation to embark on the journey where God's voice is normal and where responding to His voice in a lifestyle of obedience becomes natural. This book will take the reader into a realm of supernatural encounters that only God's grace can orchestrate. This story, like the author, is authentic, non-religious, practical, and powerful.

Brian, both a pastor and teacher for many years, has been a gift to the body of Christ. He has been an invaluable blessing to us here at Bethel in Redding. He has opened up the scriptures, helping people to have life-changing encounters with God. He is a true student of the Word, and teaches with both insight and authority. Many have been changed as Brian has walked them through the Word of God to discover what God has planned for the average believer today. His story brings hope ... abundant hope. In *Hunger Driven* Brian personally imparts the grace on his life, sharing in a very warm and inviting way what it looked like for him to be drawn out of his theological comfort zone by the Holy Spirit and begin to say "yes" to and navigate the mysterious ways of God.

I absolutely love Brian Nickens and his entire family. They are some of the most genuine and powerful believers I've had the privilege of knowing. Brian's life is one big God message. He re-presents Jesus in such and authentic and powerful way. I am thankful for the day God brought him and his family into our lives. We are better for it. His God journey has been encouraging and inspirational. I commend to you both the man and his message, Hunger Driven.

Bill Johnson
Bethel Church – Redding, CA
Author of When Heaven Invades Earth

Introduction

Lessons From The Land Of Shinar

One gentleman jumped up in surprise as the swollen lump behind his kneecap deflated in his hand while another man in the back row shouted, "the pain just left my neck, I can move my head freely". On the ground in front of me were two young women who came to the gathering because they heard it was going to be a healing service. They weren't confessing Christians, but as it turned out they had more faith than anyone else in the room. They came expecting a miracle. One girl had just then had a row of what she described as "very painful cysts" along the right side of her breast completely disappear in a moment. The other young woman had collapsed to the floor praising Jesus. I had just told a demonic spirit to leave her body, and apparently it did. Then the power of God overwhelmed her as the Holy Spirit rushed in to fill the void. She had come forward for prayer for a chronic stabbing sensation in her stomach and side. She said the doctors were having trouble diagnosing her. I realized something was wrong when I was talking to her and I noticed her right eye would stray as if it were operating independent of the other eye. I decided to call it out as a demonic spirit to see if it would respond. As I rebuked it in the name of Jesus it moved down to her left side and began inflicting the girl with sharp stabbing pains again. I rebuked it again and it moved down into her right leg and began tormenting her leg with pain. I asked the pastor of the church who was standing with me to grab her leg below the knee with both hands and choke off the circulation because I had the spirit on the run and I didn't want it to go down into her foot. He reluctantly knelt down and did what I asked. I rebuked the demonic spirit again in the name of Jesus to leave the girls body. She was cringing in pain but totally receptive to what I was doing. Within seconds it came rushing out of her body through her mouth taking all of her oxygen with it. I could feel the atmosphere shift in the room like a supernatural sonic boom. That is when the cysts disappeared in the girl next to her and she dropped to the ground and instantly began to worship God as the power of His presence began to fill the room. As both of them knelt there on the ground with much enthusiasm thanking the Lord for healing them others in the room were also touched by the presence of God as pain was leaving their bodies. All of this happened in one single moment. A group of about 25 people experienced instant and sudden healing. The exact moment the demonic spirit left everyone was touched by His power. I cant explain why or how it happened the way it did. All I know is it happened, just the way I described. The next day the pastor told me that wasn't the direction they wanted to go with their ministry. This was only the second time I had ever conducted a healing service and it ended up just like the first. God moved with great power; healing and delivering those who were desperate for His touch, yet the church leadership and a few others were offended at what *God did.* I quickly learned that healing the sick and casting out demons offends most

churches. This is common. I am ashamed to say that for many years I was among the offended.

My heart aches at the level of division and disunity that has grown in the church of Jesus Christ over the issue of healing and deliverance and various other manifestations of the presence of God. I can understand to a degree a certain level of healthy skepticism, but when demonized people are set free and their life takes on a new and positive turn for the better, and the people who are suffering from sickness and disease are healed in Jesus name, and the church is still offended? Well, that is wrong!

Many of my personal friends, some of which I have known for years have taken issue with my theological transfer into the supernatural lifestyle. Even though I am faithful to my wife and family, attend my church regularly, love the Lord with all my heart, pray, read my bible, support and participate in missions and outreach, all for the glory of God, but! Because I regularly post online testimonies of miracles and deliverances and stories of unusual manifestations of Gods presence, all of which are true and unembellished, they are concerned that I have strayed from sound biblical doctrine.

You can consider this book an apologetic in defense of the biblical accuracy of the supernatural lifestyle. Not for the sake of being proven right, nor do I have a vindictive bone in my body. But rather for the sake of the sick and dying, the lost and demonized and for the sake of the millions of Christians around the world who are sick and tired of defeat.

One of the most unique and fascinating stories of Bible history is the Tower of Babel. After the great flood humanity began to repopulate in a plain in the Land of Shinar. And there they built a tower. [1]According to Jewish historian Flavius Josephus the tower of Babel was built in direct disobedience to God. Under the leadership of the mighty hunter Nimrod the people rebelled against Gods command to venture out into the world and establish colonies. Instead they built a tower that would supposedly protect them from another flood. They hunkered down against His will.

Genesis 11:1-2, The whole earth was of one language and of one speech. As they traveled from the east, they found a plain in the land of Shinar, and they lived there.

Genesis 11:4, They said, "Come, let's build ourselves a city, and a tower whose top reaches to the sky, and let's make a name for ourselves, lest we be scattered abroad on the surface of the whole earth."

What I find most fascinating in this story is not the fact that humanity so quickly rebelled in such a grand manor, but rather I am fascinated by a comment that

---

[1] Antiquities of the Jews, Book 1, Chapter 4

God Himself makes about this rebellious group of stick-in-the-mud people. Lets read on.

5-6, Yahweh came down to see the city and the tower, which the children of men built. Yahweh said, "Behold, they are one people, and they all have one language, and this is what they begin to do. Now nothing will be withheld from them, which they intend to do.

If I am reading this correctly the Lord is stating that their unified determination, even in the context of rebellion and disobedience to God has the potential to position them for success in anything they intend to do. God intervenes.

7-9, Come, let's go down, and there confuse their language, that they may not understand one another's speech." So Yahweh scattered them abroad from there on the surface of all the earth. They stopped building the city. Therefore its name was called Babel, because there Yahweh confused the language of all the earth. From there, Yahweh scattered them abroad on the surface of all the earth.

Hidden within this story is a hint to you and I of the power of unity itself. Even though their agenda was evil and defiant the raw unity of mind, will and purpose had the power to forge and temper an unstoppable force upon the earth to the extent of demanding Gods direct and swift intervention.

With that in mind let's read:

Ephesians 4:11-16. He gave some to be apostles; and some, prophets; and some, evangelists; and some, shepherds and teachers; for the perfecting of the saints, to the work of serving, to the building up of the body of Christ; until we all attain to the unity of the faith, and of the knowledge of the Son of God, to a full grown man, to the measure of the stature of the fullness of Christ; that we may no longer be children, tossed back and forth and carried about with every wind of doctrine, by the trickery of men, in craftiness, after the wiles of error; but speaking truth in love, we may grow up in all things into him, who is the head, Christ; from whom all the body, being fitted and knit together through that which every joint supplies, according to the working in measure of each individual part, makes the body increase to the building up of itself in love.

Notice Paul said; *"until we all attain to the unity of the faith"*. Is it possible that the future of the church and our corporate effectiveness and manifest full potential has a precondition not yet met? If this is the case, which I think it is, then our best days are yet to come. This also means the responsibility for this blessed and unified future is on our end. The Lord has done His part and now we must do ours. I am not insinuating that we can operate apart from grace, but I am intrigued and hopeful that when the church achieves the Lords desired unity we will finally experience the real and raw potential of the grace that has been imparted to us.

The lesson learned in the Land of Shinar is not that God hates large-scale building projects or the idea of people wanting to stick together. The lesson learned is that when unity is harnessed, intentional and channeled, it is unstoppable. In the case of Babel, God had to disperse them, not just because they were unified. They were unified under the wrong spirit that was motivating them to settle against the will of God when it was time to venture out and fill the earth.

I hope that the content of this book helps us the Church find our way towards the kind of unity that deems all things possible for the glory and the honor of our Lord Jesus Christ. I believe there is an expression of the church that has yet to be seen on this planet. It may even have its own sound and its own language. I don't believe we know yet what it looks like nor do we know the potential of it. But it's out there and our mandate is to discover it. The road is paved with great exploits for the glory of God. Influence in the power centers of the world, favor with cities and governments, signs and wonders, miracles, healings and deliverance will be our calling card and our unity will cause the enemy to tremble and quake like never before. And just like the people of Babel, nothing will be withheld from us, which we intend to do. And the response from heaven will be in support and favor.

The script for this is writ on the pages of the Bible and the tablets of our heart. Lets not let the people of the Land Of Shinar go down as the most unified people group in history. If their defiance-based unity can initiate a response from heaven that disables them, imagine what can happen when a God-approved unity is achieved and realized in the church. Heaven will respond with a seal of approval and a deployment of assisting and ministering angel's unprecedented. This is not just a hope but I believe its is an inevitability.

The victims of this world's prince desperately need the church to rise up in love and humility tapping into the supernatural power that is available to each and every one of us.

Now to him who is able to do exceedingly abundantly above all that we ask or think, according to the power that works in us. Ephesians 3:20

We can do this!

1. Hearing

The restaurant was not too busy. I had never eaten there before, but the décor was inviting and the menu was appealing so I gave it a whirl. My waitress was very inquisitive, and after multiple questions about who I was and where I was from, I finally told her I was passing through on a speaking engagement for a local church. She looked very surprised. I'm not very pastoral looking. My head is shaved, I was wearing skinny jeans and a t-shirt, and both my arms are covered with tattoos. I didn't fit the profile of a traveling preacher.

She quickly responded, "I don't believe in God, I only believe in things I can prove." To her surprise I was totally unaffected by her statement. I matter-of-factly said something like, "that's cool." I placed my order, and all was well between us. About ten minutes later, she returned with my order. It looked good: pan-fried garlic shrimp in a bed of fresh pasta. She knew I was impressed by this presentation, especially in such a small and inconspicuous restaurant.

Before she walked away from my table I asked her "why are you leaving town?" Her face went from an ear-to-ear smile to dead cold and bug-eyed. She leaned into my table and under her breath said, "How did you know? I haven't told anybody,"

Without hesitation, I said: "the God you don't believe in just told me, and He wants you to know that if you stay in this city, the very things you hope and dream for will come to pass."

That recent incident in the restaurant was a long time coming. Hearing directly from God in such a precise manner wasn't always my norm.

Flash back to 1989. My wife and I had taken our two children, Kristen and Austin, to Disneyland for the day. Our home was only a few blocks away, and—on occasion when the weather was real nice and we knew it would be un-crowded (comparatively speaking)—we would clear the day's schedule, drop everything and keep the kids out of school to head for "The Happiest Place on Earth." As usual we had a wonderful day walking through the Magic Kingdom, enjoying the creativity and genius of Walt Disney. Our perfect day ended with the perfect encore: the amazing and always enjoyable Main Street Electrical Parade. If you haven't seen this incredible display of lights and marching bands along with the larger-than-life cast of Disney characters, you must. Add it to your bucket list of things to do before you….. uh… whatever.

The parade is the last event of the evening for the Disney Park, so the crowd flows onto the street, following the tail of the parade toward the exit. It is like one big happy family streaming out of the park with smiles and gladness. The children are happy with armloads of Disney toys and candy, the parents are happy (if three hundred bucks poorer), and Mickey, Goofy, and Cinderella have a spring in their

step as they close out another blissful day in the kingdom.

As we approached the end of Main Street, just about 100 yards before the exit, the elderly woman in front of me suddenly fell to the ground and hit her head on the pavement. I could hear the sound of her skull smack the ground. I stopped and knelt down to assist her as people gathered around to see what happened. Within seconds, the Disney medical staff was on the spot, ready to take over and assist the woman, who was in a bit of shock as blood ran down her face. She was fully conscious, and her wound was small, but there was a lot of blood. In that moment, I could hear a voice inside of me saying, "Be healed in Jesus Name." An immediate urge to say those words rose up from within, as I stood there, paralyzed and silent.

But I did nothing.

I had never healed anyone in my life. Yes, I was a practicing Christian, but the impulse to heal a person in public or in private was strange to me. There had been occasions in my past when a friend or family member had become ill or diagnosed with a disease that would prompt me to *pray* for their healing. But those prayers were always voiced with great sentiment and belief in God's ability to heal—never with expectation that He actually *would*. In fact when and if I had ever prayed for a miracle, I had placed all the responsibility on the sick person, asking God to give them the strength to endure their season of trial that (in my opinion back then) had been allowed by

God's sovereign will as a way of drawing them closer to Him. The miracle I prayed for was for them to have supernatural strength to suffer. Looking back, I now realize what a ridiculous prayer that is. I was actually adding to their burden and sealing them into their condition. And since they typically didn't know any better, they too would nod in affirmation, determined to embrace their cross of infirmity.

But then there was that day at Disneyland? The inner voice said, "Be healed in Jesus Name." Where had that come from? Certainly it did not come from me. I remember telling my wife, Doreen, about it as we continued walking out of the park. At the time, we both agreed that it would be great for that to happen, but of course neither of us actually knew what to do about it, nor did we ponder the idea beyond that moment.

Over the next few years, I would often recall that voice. The memory of it was so profoundly embedded in my mind because the inner voice that spoke that night had shouted with volume and clarity, and it came from a distinct place, another realm than all my other thoughts. It was like an unused portion of my brain had awakened to an external voice. From then on, my mind was hooked on this idea, this notion: Is it possible that I could actually say those words, "Be healed in Jesus Name," and the person would actually receive a miracle? Could it be that simple? It was as if the words themselves were more than random thoughts or impulse. The words felt as though they carried their

own power to accomplish their own will. I knew this was no ordinary thought or impulse.

My understanding at the time was that the voice of God primarily came in the form of conviction and persuasion towards right decision-making. And then there was the added, inherited belief that reading the Bible discovers the majority of God's thoughts, ideas, and will. Even though I studied the Bible and attended a solid, Bible-teaching church, was it possible I was missing something? Was there a frequency in my spirituality I wasn't aware of?

I believe that within every Christian on the face of the earth there is embedded a desire to witness, live in, and be a recipient of the supernatural power of God. Within all of God's children sounds an inner voice. It speaks from what I like to call the "God channel" of our consciousness. It even physically touches a certain part of our brain. Not only can we hear this voice, sometimes we can even feel the vibration of the sound and tell from what direction and angle it came. This is the voice that calls us into our destiny. This is the voice that leads us beyond the realm of intellectual ascent to certain creeds and doctrine and on into the realm of mystery, awe, and supernatural living. The entire movement of Jesus Christ is being drawn gently into this realm of the Spirit. The realm where all matter is subject to the will of God. The realm where the command of faith has final say, and creation itself must succumb to the voice of the trusted ones. You and I are the trusted ones. Those who call Jesus Lord have been entrusted to be the ambassadors of His will, the voice of His commands, and the hands of His work. Yes, the work of God's hands has become the hands of God's work. And that voice you hear is Him taking command.

Will you obey the voice? I am talking about a quality of Christian living that is beyond principals and bullet-point sermons. I am not talking about how to conquer sin and overcome temptation. Those are the byproducts of this lifestyle, not the focus. Nor am I talking about discovering your gifts or ministry calling. I am talking about the raw, supernatural power and the stewardship of that power. A resource that has yet to be fully realized on the earth, but is about to be unleashed in unprecedented measure on and through you and me. Our only mandate is to obey the voice of God and watch Him do incredible things.

"Why do you call me, 'Lord, Lord, 'and don't do the things which I say?" Luke 6:46

2. Voice Activated

After Christ ascended into heaven and the Holy Spirit had descended upon the 120 Christ followers in Jerusalem during the [2]Feast of Pentecost, all kinds of strange phenomena began to happen in the lives of the Jesus people. The Spirit of God began to flow freely and powerfully in and through anyone who would yield to Him. No longer were the people of God dependent solely on the few prophets who acted as the voice of God. Individuals were now *voice activated* by the Lord Himself. The New Testament is filled with detailed accounts of God speaking directly to those who would listen. When Saul was literally struck down by the power of God on the road to Damascus, he and those with him heard the voice of God. Saul was led to Damascus as a blind man where he met a man named Ananias, who had also heard the voice of God telling him about Saul and asking Ananias to go out and find Saul and lay hands on him to receive his sight back. Reading on into the next chapter of Acts, we find Peter in a trance on a rooftop in the town of Joppa. Peter also heard the voice of God telling him to "kill and eat." This open-heaven encounter was the very event God used to transform Peter's mind and give him clarity and understanding as to God's desire that the entire Gentile (non-Jew) world be included in this new,

---

[2] Read the Book Of Acts

universal outpouring of God's Holy Spirit. From this moment on, Peter became a spokesperson for the Gentile world and a witness that the Holy Spirit was liberal and free to all who open their hearts to Jesus, repent, and are baptized. No longer was the Mosaic covenant of sacrificial law necessary for relationship with God. God was now close and personal and *speaking to all who will hear His voice*. This revelation became a bone of contention and division within the religious community; no longer were they the sole proprietors of God's Kingdom.

It is this same dynamic that has yet to be fully realized within the Church today. God is speaking directly to *you* the commands of His will and even the specific instructions on how to represent Him in any given moment. We still have a tendency to be over-dependent on *the man of God.* But, as John Wimber so eloquently put it with the title of his book: *Everybody Gets to Play.* Jesus said: *"My sheep hear My voice, and I know them and they follow Me".* [3]

After Jesus had already ascended to heaven, He actually spoke *from* heaven *to* the apostle John saying:

"Behold I stand at the door and knock: if anyone hears my voice, and open the door, then I will come in to him, and will dine with him, and he with me"
Revelation 3:20

---

[3] John 10:27

Jesus wasn't saying this to unbelievers as an invitation to be saved. He was speaking this to the already believing church of Laodicea. They had become lukewarm and overly dependent on their resources and obviously unable to hear the voice of Jesus anymore.

The introduction into the supernatural lifestyle that the Lord wants for all who follow Him begins with the ability to hear the voice of God. The miraculous starts with the voice. Hearing this voice—the Word of God—is different than the ability to read His Word or memorize scripture. Hearing this voice is not the same as adhering to biblical principal or sound doctrine. Those things are good, but those things are all done in the natural realm. Reading, memorizing, self-discipline, and applying biblical truths are all great and necessary attributes for the Christian. But! I am talking about the *actual* voice of God spoken in *real* time. The voice that calls from the God-place of our consciousness in a specific moment with clarity—often in contrast to our current mental landscape and current train of thought. This voice comes like a ray of light piercing the atmosphere of our mind and landing in that *certain place* that only God can touch. I like to think of this as the region of grey matter real estate that He has reserved for Himself. This voice is not solicited or conjured up. It just comes, and we know it is from Him.

That is the voice I am talking about.

When we become tuned to *that* voice, then we become like the horse with a supple mouth—a tool in the hands of our creator, an agent of the Almighty, ready to do the things He says. But we must learn to hear His voice and distinguish it from all other voices and thoughts, and then we must act, trusting and knowing that it is He. It is this kind of relationship with God that develops into a miraculous lifestyle because we can do nothing apart from Him. Jesus said, *"If you remain in me and my words remain in you, you will ask whatever you desire and it will be done for you." John 15:7*

He wasn't just referring to His written word from the Bible. He is referring to His voice that speaks directly to you now. This is the voice that says things like, "Go tell that person their child is going to be okay," even though that person is a complete stranger. The same voice tells you exactly how to minister to the sick with instructions like, "Tell them to bend over and touch their toes," even though the lower vertebrae in their spine are fused together. This voice from heaven is able to speak the very will of God with great precision. Some of you are hearing that voice even now as the Holy Spirit is beginning to activate your mind. Trust what you are hearing and act accordingly. Miracles will happen. It really is that simple.

3. If It's God, I Want It

It was late Sunday evening, and we had just returned from church. We were getting ready for bed and discussing the church service. My wife and I were still in our transition phase of crossing over from our previous mainstream evangelical Christian underpinnings into the revival culture of Bethel Redding. Because we had been trained to be extremely cautious of the charismatic movement, it was difficult for us to be totally objective in the new environment around us.

That particular evening, there was quite a buzz because [4]Heidi Baker was the guest speaker. Heidi's obvious love and compassion for people, especially orphaned children, was infectious. My wife Doreen is particularly compassionate when it comes to children and babies. So right away I could tell that Heidi was winning her over. I was already committed in my heart to this new breed of believers at Bethel, but Doreen was still on the fence. She wasn't opposed to it or critical at all. Her hesitancy had more to do with the dynamics between her and me. Our entire married life, I have been adventurous and risky. Starting businesses, buying and selling homes, speculating real estate, planting churches, moving to new cities, taking up new sports and activities, etc,

---

[4] See irisglobal.org

etc, etc. By default she has had to become our voice of reason. And this matter of spirituality and God's kingdom was by far the most important for us both. She wasn't about to be dragged into a theological shift unless she knew it was God doing the dragging. And for that I applaud and thank her. Over the years, her caution has served as a foundation and safety net for us on many occasions.

But then there was Heidi. Wow! That night, as she spoke from the Bethel pulpit, our hearts came alive with passion and compassion. Our love for God was elevated to new heights, and the joy on Heidi's countenance was no doubt the joy of the Lord. But! At the same time, we were challenged with these awkward manifestations that we weren't use to. As Heidi spoke about her ministry and experiences in Mozambique, she often just dropped to the ground, mid-sentence, and acted drunk in the spirit, drifting off into what I will call I-love-You-Jesus-land. What was up with that? On top of that, her husband, Roland, would wander around down by the front of the stage laying hands on people, and they would drop to the ground in piles, laughing and some of them shaking. Everything we had been warned about and had become suspicious of as carnal and false was happening right in front of us, while at the same time our hearts were laid wide open and raw in the power of Heidi's presence and the penetrating truth and love she spoke in. The Holy Spirit had ambushed us.

It was never our idea to even move to Redding and certainly not to leave behind our previous church

family and affiliation. We had no defense against full-blown love and manifest joy. I knew Doreen was scared...but we both liked it. I found myself wanting to join the people on the ground laughing. They were having a good time. And their joy did not interfere at all with Heidi's message. The love of God was saturating the room as she spoke.

We drove to our nearby home in shock. As we were getting ready for bed, I—in my typical fashion—needed to come to some kind of conclusion before going to sleep. It was no doubt a where-do-we-go-from-here moment. Doreen prefers to ponder for days, and I prefer to decide and move forward. It was in that tension and under the influence of Heidi's infectious love for Jesus that the Lord synced up our hearts to His, and Doreen trusted me to lead the way. Although we were not able to reconcile all that we had experienced that evening, we could not deny the very presence of God. The question was no longer what we thought or believed about the evening, the question was: what is God thinking? Yet God was not telling us right away. We had to embrace mystery! Our typical method of chapter-and-verse Bible confirmation was not an option because we didn't know what chapter or what verse to turn to. Our minds were clouded with biases and pet doctrines from the past. It's not that Scripture didn't confirm all that we had experienced that night, we just didn't know how to approach Scripture in this context. Our Bibles were underlined in all the wrong places. Heidi and Roland Baker knew something about God's Word and the Holy Spirit that we didn't know. We wanted what they had. And for the first time in a long time we had to trust our heart.

He brought me to the banquet hall, and His banner over me is love. Song of Songs 2:4

We realized we were going to have to leave behind the comfort blanket of what we thought was perfect theology of *decent-and-in-order-ism* and step into a new spiritual journey of perpetual pondering and trust. We recalled the very circumstances that had led us to this crossroads and reminded ourselves that the only reason we were there was because we had been following the Lord's lead. He certainly wouldn't lead us into a dead end and then set us up for deception. It was in that raw, bare moment of willingness to embrace mystery that I said, "All I know is, if it's God, I want it." We went to sleep pondering.

4. Living Beyond Comprehension

Without controversy, the mystery of godliness is great.
1 Timothy 3:16

One of most subtle cruelties in the Church today is intellectually driven Christianity. It is possible and common to mistake mental stimulation for Holy Spirit inspiration. There is a vast difference between Scripture revealed and Scripture remembered. That is why hearing God's voice and recognizing its sound—and even the place in our mind it often lands—is so crucial. This may or may not come as a surprise to some of you, but it is possible to preach what appears to be a biblically sound sermon that is completely detached from the heart of God in that moment. I have come to a place in my own spiritual journey where, if I don't like what I am hearing or reading, I don't care how many Bible verses speakers stack on top of their ideas, I don't receive their messages into my heart. On the other hand, I can hear a sermon or a teaching that I don't fully comprehend in the moment, but my heart comes alive at what I am hearing. There is life on the words as they are spoken, and the Holy Spirit within in me is responding, saying, "Yes, yes."

Trust in Yahweh with all your heart; and don't lean on your own understanding. In all your ways acknowledge him, and he will make your paths straight. Don't be wise in your own eyes. Prov 3:5-7

If our intellectual pursuit of Bible knowledge does not lead us into experiences equivalent to those we read about in Scripture, we become a spawning ground for the spirit of religion and a playground for demons. The demonic realm knows that churches and ministries who pride themselves in doctrinal purity and their supposedly solid, biblical foundations tend to be powerless when it comes to ousting spiritual forces from their midst, so the demons settle in. I have witnessed this dynamic first hand.

These same churches have no healing ministry, either. Though they can offer all kinds of food and moral support for the tormented, sick and dying, yet they offer no power to heal or deliver them. Not only does this form of Christianity facilitate and empower human pride, it also kills the creativity and spontaneity that are crucial for the supernatural power of God to be manifest and realized. Even the unbelieving and pagans have pointed out the creative suppression and arrogance of rigid Christianity in its many forms and colors.

If you desire a Christian experience that continually increases in anointing, power, victory and supernatural manifestations then you must ditch all preconceived notions about what God can and cannot do. You must open yourself up to things you don't understand and consider the idea that your theology and doctrine may not be as sound as you think they are. They may be safe, but not sound. The good news that Jesus preached and demonstrated was

not safe! It was beyond current comprehension, and for that He was hated. But the results were undeniable. Even Jesus deferred to the miraculous works as the proof to validate His identity:

"If I don't do the works of my Father, don't believe me. But if I do them, though you don't believe me, believe the works; that you may know and believe that the Father is in me. John 10:38-39

To abide in Christ, and to have His words abide in you, is to live in the realm of mystery. Much of what is labeled "perfect theology" is a deception and an illusion created by those who think they have it. If it has no power over sickness, demons, and death, then it is bad theology. This doesn't mean everyone has to have a worldwide healing ministry. It does mean that when you personally encounter sickness, death, and the demonic you have the authority to do something about it. Do you go hard after a miracle, commanding bodies to be healed like Jesus did, or commanding demons to leave, like Jesus did? Or do you excuse yourself from the confrontation and then wrap your inaction in other Bible verses to make yourself feel better? All the while, the people whom the Lord has appointed for you to help as His ambassador remain sick, tormented, and dying. This is not the way of agape!

I have discovered that most believers who don't attempt to heal the sick are fearful that if the person doesn't get healed, then it derails the faith of the sick person and makes them more confused. That is ridiculous. I've never seen that happen, and I have attempted to minister healing in the name of Jesus hundreds of times. Some were healed and some were not. But all of them are thankful that someone had the guts to try, especially those who are terminal. They are so desperate as they lay dying. They just hope someone will come along and at least try. This means we have to be willing to put our own reputation on the line, not allowing offense to settle in to our hearts when and if a person we pray for doesn't get healed.

One Sunday evening I was speaking in a church where the congregation had been told to come expecting healing and miracles. I was totally fine with that because I wanted to see some healing miracles myself. Two women arrived in wheelchairs and set themselves in the very front row. One was a middle-aged woman whose body was paralyzed with a crippling disease. I can't remember exactly what was ailing her. The other was a young girl in her early twenties that had lost her legs below the knee in a car accident. As the evening escalated a measure a faith came over me and in front of the entire church I stepped down off the stage and spoke with absolute clarity that the will of God is that these women be healed. I proceeded to minister to each one of them individually, commanding their bodies to heal in the name of Jesus. I placed my hands on the shoulder of the girl whose legs were severed and commanded her legs to heal in Jesus Name. Neither of them walked out their wheelchair that night. And neither of them was offended or embarrassed by me pointing them out. After the ministry time ended I sat down with each of them and continued praying with them. Both of them expressed a deep gratitude. The girl whose legs were severed began to cry as she thanked me. She said that no one has ever made such a bold attempt on her behalf and for that she was thankful and given a new sense of hope. Some may choose to criticize me and feel validated because, after all, those girls did note rise up and walk. I suggest that those critics may be the problem! Is it possible that the breakthrough that we need to see these kinds of miracles is dependent on our corporate unity on this matter? The church we read about in the Book of Acts had only one theology for healing. It was based on the ministry of Jesus Christ and therefore in their mind healing was not an issue. I am positive they couldn't imagine a Christianity that wasn't proven by signs wonders and miracles. The church has actually fallen from its initial platform and has become less than what Christ died for. But it can and will be restored. As for me, I will continue to attempt to heal every person whom the Lord asks me to. Thus far I have been personally involved in a couple hundred healings, not to mention the hundreds upon hundreds I have witnessed in my own church. If we don't step out in faith, even at the risk of nothing happening, then nothing will ever happen in the realm of healing and miracles. This is not acceptable.

The whole point of this book is to encourage you to hear God's voice and do what He says. To step into what I know your heart already desires. If Christ the healer already dwells within you, yield to Him, and you will leave a trail of miracles. It's very rare to see the miracle, because *most* miracles that are external happen in such a way that you miss the visual pleasure of watching the transformation. Sometimes, a miracle is progressive. You plant the seed, and over days or weeks, it blossoms into a full healing. All the while God has performed a beautiful work in another person through you.

Our job is to simply obey His voice and believe. The miracles will follow. I cannot count the number of miracles that have happened in the aftermath of my own personal ministry. I have discovered that most healings aren't fully realized or acknowledged until days or weeks later.

"They went out, and preached everywhere, the Lord working with them, and confirming the word by the signs that followed them. Amen. Mark 16:20

5. I'm Okay, You're Okay

I am hoping and believing that up to this point in time, the Lord has been working mysteriously in your life, drawing you out of your comfort zone theologically speaking. It is this mysterious journey and the unanswered questions stemming from it that have drawn you to this book. You want clarity and need answers, but God is moving you along more quickly than you have time to reorganize your thoughts. It's possible that your dream life has taken on a unique twist of biblical proportions. Some of you are praying with more passion and desperation hoping for a dramatic shift in your spiritual life. Some miracles and unusual incidents may be happening around you, and you are not quite sure how or why. Trust me when I say: You are on the right track. As you move forward on this quest you are stirring up the supernatural unseen realm around you. This very dynamic is happening to hundreds of thousands of believers all around the world—even in America where the mainstream culture of Christianity has become resistant to the move of the Holy Spirit, especially if it is accompanied by unusual behavior. Fortunately God is releasing more of His Kingdom here on earth because a large enough portion of the church has finally asked Him to do so. So get ready for an amazing but expensive future. Expensive? Yes, expensive. It will cost you everything. In return you will gain the *one* thing. God—like you've never known Him.

Brothers, I don't regard myself as yet having taken hold, but one thing I do. Forgetting the things which are behind, and stretching forward to the things which are before, I press on toward the goal for the prize of the high calling of God in Christ Jesus. Let us therefore, as many as are perfect, think this way. If in anything you think otherwise, God will also reveal that to you. Philippians 3:13-15

The question that begs an answer: How do I respond-to and navigate-through the mysterious realm of Godliness if I am being moved along beyond my ability to confirm every single thing with Scripture as it is happening?

First you must learn to trust. Trust whom? Yourself. You have God within you, after all. If your pursuit is a noble pursuit and you are truly seeking after God, then you are on the right track. Go ahead and trust yourself and the voice you hear. Forget about what others might think. It isn't their job to work out your salvation; it's your job. Don't let fear control you.

Unfortunately, much of what is called discipleship is the exact opposite and there is so much unhealthy language in the Church that has become self-flagellating and mutilating. It is well accepted in churchy environments to believe "I am nothing and God is everything," or "I am just a sinner saved by grace." I could go on and on with these one-liners that have been spouted from the pews of testimony for decades. I have heard them all my life. I even used to say them myself.

What is wrong with this picture: Jesus handed over the keys to the kingdom and all power and all authority to His disciples. Subsequently they modeled His ministry and demonstrated His power. And now, all these years later Christianity at large is notorious for branding any believer or group that attempts to publically demonstrate the power of God by healing the sick or casting out devils, or speak words of knowledge or prophesy as New Age and demonic. Then we create doctrines and eschatology's that make the devil out to be the most powerful and dominant force on the planet. Even though Satan was defeated at the cross. So, instead of making disciples, we shun those who try to act like an authentic New Testament disciple. They are labeled and disempowered via public skepticism, accusatory cut and pasted You Tube Video's, theological blogs and websites that are laced through-out with mountains of bible verses and doctrinal positions and quotations from early church fathers condemning those who dare to claim the healing power of Jesus or to be prophets or operate in the supernatural realm.

And lets not forget the most powerful demonic weapon in the church today. Those perfectly worded, wrapped in pseudo humility underhanded innuendos of slight criticisms and indirect finger pointing from the pulpits across the land, week after week after week. All this is justified under the banner of defending truth and so-called sound doctrine. It makes me sick writing about it.

It's time to trust yourself and your motives. You need the power of God to manifest in your life. Don't say 'I am nothing', because *you are something*. I understand you have trusted God for salvation and may have come out of self-serving and pleasure-seeking lifestyles into the comfort of Gods grace. But He did not mean for you to spend the rest of your life sitting in a pew on Sundays, listening to sermon after sermon of regurgitated renditions of doctrines of grace. Don't get me wrong; these are good things to work through. These are basic Christian attributes of our faith but not the culmination of our life's work. We are meant to live a Jesus lifestyle of supernatural power and anointing. It is our job to prophecy destinies, speak words of knowledge, hold back storms, heal diseases, and cast out demons and to demonstrate the power of God. And if you aren't getting the desired results keep learning and trying until something happens. It will happen.

I once stood in a hailstorm in front of a crowd of people at a Christian music festival and commanded the hail to stop in the Name of Jesus. And it did, within seconds. On another occasion I was speaking to a group of young people at a summer camp. The moment I began to teach a hailstorm started pounding the metal roof where we were gathered. The hails stones were huge and the sound was so loud that it overpowered my voice even though I was speaking through a microphone. I bowed my head and prayed aloud, "dear Lord make it stop". The storm stopped immediately. It went from a massive hailstorm to zero in a split second. That is normal Christianity.

So let us stop going over the basic teachings about Christ again and again. Let us go on instead and become mature in our understanding. Surely we don't need to start again with the fundamental importance of repenting from evil deeds and placing our faith in God. You don't need further instruction about baptisms, the laying on of hands, the resurrection of the dead, and eternal judgment. And so, God willing, we will move forward to further understanding. Hebrews 6:1-3

When we are committed to—and open up ourselves to—this kind of Christianity, the very atmospheres that are charged with the power of God's presence cause people to do unusual things—mysterious things that change the texture and the composure of our corporate gatherings. And just like any other gathering of God's people, not everything that happens is of God, but most of it is. It follows that some of the mystery you will have to embrace is filled with behavior that you don't understand yet. I have discovered that what has been traditionally written off as hyper-emotionalism and false manifestations can be real, bonafied God moments. When I first started attending Bethel Church in Redding there was a person in particular who really annoyed me. I didn't know them personally. I was afraid to talk to them. They were constantly shaking their head and dipping and flinching during prayer and during worship. They would clinch one fist in the air and shake their head side to side with one foot lifted off the ground. I assumed that they were trying to conjure up the Holy Ghost and decided that it was all for show to look spiritual. One day I was sitting at the church relaxing and reading my Bible when this person randomly came over to me and knelt down in front of me and started speaking words of knowledge about my life and my journey. She knew all about my recent past and the life journey I was on. Then she proceeded to speak powerful words of encouragement and confirmation about the very things I had recently been praying about. Then she got up and walked away in her usual unusual manner dipping and jerking as she went. My heart melted instantly and I was so blessed by her words. She spoke from heaven directly to me as if she was an angel sent to deliver a message. I repented for my judgmental attitude and critical outlook, and vowed to never again judge another person's actions and mannerisms in the house of God.

A mystery within the mystery is: how can God be touching one person so powerfully and yet the person right next to them, possibly you, is experiencing nothing? I highly recommend Che Ahn's book, *Say Goodbye To Powerless Christianity* and John Arnott's book *Manifestations and Prophetic Symbolism in a Move of the Spirit*. Both of these men and their wives have come through the journey of embracing the mystery of how God works and have lived to tell about it. Ha, ha! They offer great comfort and tangible proof of God's powerful involvement in what their critics believed was—and what they

labeled as—deceptive and un-biblical behavior and manifestations. Yet, all the while, souls and more souls have been entering into the kingdom of God as a result. Miracles and healing are taking place. People are being commissioned and sent out all over the world, preaching the gospel, healing the sick, casting out demons, and transforming entire cities and regions. And these bizarre manifestations and moves of God continue to effectively release the kingdom of God all over the world. All because the men and women at the helm of these ministries embraced the mystery around them, took note of what God was doing in their midst, and treasured the fruit of His works even if they didn't fully understand it. Which leads me to the next point.

6. The Mystery Train

An important step in this journey is to recall and even document the circumstances that brought you to this new level of desire and to continually hunger and thirst for more of God. You are now riding the "Mystery Train" and its time to Remind yourself of the dissatisfaction of the past and, if applicable, even the present condition of your spiritual life. In doing so, you will realize that God has been leading you on a very personal journey. He has been hearing and responding to the cry of your heart, drawing you gently into your destiny in Him. And when you come again into the realization that you have been hearing God's voice, *you must treasure God's mysterious words and deeds in your heart.* Write down what God has been speaking to you, and recount the events and divine, God-scented coincidences that have been increasing in your life.

It is from this vantage point of realizing that God has taken you beyond your current understanding of His ways that you can gain *better and more accurate visibility.* From this vantage point, go back into Scripture and rebuild a new arsenal of biblical confirmations and new revelations. You must allow the miraculous and often mysterious ways of God to become the lens through which you navigate Scripture. This approach flies in the face of what most of us were taught: that understanding of God's Word comes first, and then we cautiously apply what we understand to be true. Without realizing it, your faith has probably been in your intellect. The irony of this is that most people are preached into the Kingdom of God by being told that they must embrace Jesus and His salvation through faith, even though the depths of the cross and the complexities of salvation are beyond their comprehension. So we take this giant leap of faith into the mystery of God's salvation only to be funneled into atmospheres and churches that often despise the ongoing mysterious works of God. Our salvation becomes the only mystery we are allowed to acknowledge, while our actual Christian life is reduced to study, church events, and marriage lessons. Is it any wonder many leave the Church opting for personal, non-organized religion? I used to cringe when I heard statements from my non-church-attending friends like, "I don't need church. I experience God on the mountain tops when I hunt." I realize now some of them were right. Their church experience wasn't nearly as spiritual as their personal God encounters were in nature. The Church often becomes like a tree that kills its own fruit. Jesus said;

"But woe to you, scribes and Pharisees, hypocrites! Because you shut up the Kingdom of Heaven against men; for you don't enter in yourselves, neither do you allow those who are entering in to enter. Matthew 23:14

Notice that Jesus said they "shut up the kingdom of heaven." Many ministries today do the exact same thing. They open the doors of the church, extend a hand of brotherly love and fellowship, but shut up the kingdom of heaven. The Church is not the kingdom. It is *in* the kingdom but not the *total* sum of the kingdom. Unfortunately it is possible to be active in the church and in ministry yet be totally oblivious to the supernatural attributes of the kingdom of heaven. And in many cases intentionally kept from the manifest power and presence of God. One reason so many Christians feel spiritually dry is because they have been in the Church for so long, but they haven't been seeing the evidence of the kingdom of heaven. Signs, wonders, and miracles are all attributes of the kingdom of heaven. The Church can be rigid and predictable, though the kingdom of heaven we are supposed to represent is full of surprises. After all, it is a supernatural kingdom…isn't it?

Let me offer one example of how embracing mystery helped me rediscover God's Word. After about a year into this journey of supernatural Christianity I had participated-in and witnessed many unusual scenarios where God was doing things in strange and mysterious ways through His people. I had been personally involved in numerous healing miracles and had experienced many strange manifestations of God's power. I had also successfully cast demons out of people and witnessed first hand the strange occurrences that go along with the deliverance ministry. I had come to realize that just about anything is possible. One of these mysterious events occurred during a home group my wife and I hosted.

I was mentally transported to another location on the earth during a time of prayer and worship. I was taken into a prison where persecuted Christians were having a glorious worship experience from cell to cell. All of this started in my imagination, but the imagery was so real and unsolicited that I felt compelled to run with it. The images were coming from that 'God place" of my mind that I was learning to become familiar with. I was riding on the back of an angel through the prison corridors opening the prison doors, and setting the captives free. I began narrating what I was seeing, play-by-play, to the attendees in our home group. A few of the people in the room began speaking in tongues with a distinct, Chinese sounding-dialect. Others laughed, while some shook as the Holy Spirit fell on us all.

After this unusual, 30 to 40 minute encounter, we opened up a map and came to an agreement that we had been transported into a prison in Burma. The reason we chose Burma is because one of the girls in our group had recently been there, and, as I described what I saw, felt and discerned she insisted that I was in a Burmese prison. Everything was so random and spontaneous one could easily brush the entire scenario off as conjured, fake and even childish.

A few days later, to my amazement, I saw on major network news that Hilary Clinton had just returned from Burma where she was negotiating for the release of "political prisoners". In Burma, "political prisoners" actually means Christians. You can go online and read Hilary's January 13 statement in the

Treaty Room of the State Department. Concerning Burma she said, "I urged them to unconditionally release all political prisoners, halt hostilities in ethnic areas, and seek a true political settlement. This would broaden the space for political and civic activity, and by doing so, it would lay the groundwork to fully implement legislation that would *protect universal freedoms of assembly, speech, and association.*" [5]

The section I italicized is what I believe refers to the Christians right to assemble, preach and have fellowship with one another.

My heart jumped for joy as I heard the news. Just three nights prior, our little group had embraced the mystery of what we believed God was revealing to us as we literally acted out the unlocking of prison doors. It was a very bizarre, mysterious evening. It even felt strange afterward, but we knew it was God! I have no Bible study or theological confirmation for this unusual encounter. I believe that my consciousness was translated right into that prison carried on the back of an angel of the Lord. I know what I saw. I assume that in most church circles, this kind of seemingly imaginary role-play would be shunned as possibly demonic or at the least manipulative. I am convinced that our group played a significant, spiritual role as unusual intercessors helping to bring about the will of God on earth: the

---

[5] See state.gov remarks and video on Burma dated 1/13/2012
http://www.state.gov/secretary/20092013clinton/rm/2012/01/180667.htm

release of captives. Doesn't the Bible say that Jesus came *to set the captives free?* Is that statement more than just an analogy for those who are captives of sin? I think so. Now, even when I read Scriptures, I think in miraculous terms. The following comparison may seem off the subject but it does illustrate how these unusual spiritual encounters of mine have affected my bible reading. Lets read the following Psalm and I will show you what I mean.

I waited patiently for Yahweh. He turned to me, and heard my cry. He brought me up also out of a horrible pit, out of the miry clay. He set my feet on a rock, and gave me a firm place to stand. He has put a new song in my mouth, even praise to our God. Many shall see it, and fear, and shall trust in Yahweh. Psalm 40:1-3

I can easily imagine David having literally fallen into a muddy pit, possibly as a shepherd boy roaming the countryside tending his father's sheep. After hours of trying to climb out and yelling for help, he realizes his only hope is a miracle. He stops clawing and struggling, possibly from exhaustion, and he turns his heart and hope toward the Lord. Suddenly, he is lifted out of the pit by a ministering angel, and his feet are gently set on a solid rock. As he makes his way home, he begins to sing a brand new song of God's deliverance in time of trouble. This testimony from Psalm 40 doesn't have to be a metaphor or an allegory. It may very well be a literal account that spawned new revelation in David's heart that unfolds throughout the rest of the Psalm.

Until I had personally experienced the Lord in dramatic and bizarre ways—such as the prison encounter—I would have never read that Psalm this way. My supernatural lifestyle causes me to see Scripture completely different than before. My Scripture readings and interpretations are actually more literal now. I am not saying conclusively that David actually fell into a pit, but I wouldn't doubt it either. I personally lean in that direction, not just in this Psalm... in all of them! I believe David lived a rare and unusual supernatural lifestyle as a forerunner of new covenant potential. Therefore, the Psalms are prophetic templates and scripts of normal Christianity. The supernatural encounters threaded throughout the entire Bible are real and available to us today. To view the Psalms as merely allegorical poems, robs them of power...and robs you of your potential.

7. The High Ground Of Pondering

Now that you have learned to trust yourself and you have come to embrace and value the mysterious ways of God, you can *ponder what all this means* and where it might lead you. The pondering mode is where the supernatural lifestyle is sustained. "To ponder" is to meditate and evaluate your situation with a believing believers mindset. It's like sitting on a high hill after a difficult climb. From that position you can look back at the difficult path behind you, and you can look the opposite direction at the terrain that awaits you. And guess what? You can sit there for as long as you like. As long as you treasure the Lord's words and works in your heart, you will be fine. You can rest and not doubt, knowing that you are on safe ground and that God will make the next move. But take note: you can never go back. There is a point of no return in the supernatural lifestyle. The mysterious works of God and the variety of ways that His miracles are manifest have a way of keeping you in a constant state of wondering. This is a good thing.

One Sunday night at church pastor Bill Johnson asked people to stand if they were in need of breakthrough in certain areas of life and/or health. My wife Doreen stood along with a couple hundred others. As she stood there with her hands out as if to receive something her face began to tingle. When she sat back down there was gold sparkles like tiny pieces of glitter all over her face. After about 20 to 30 minutes all the gold sparkles had either dissolved or disappeared. I am not sure which? Doreen was so encouraged to know that heaven responded to her response. To this day she ponders and cherishes that moment, even though either of us can explain what it means. What we do know is that Doreen stood up to receive a breakthrough from the Lord and sat down with her face glistening with gold dust. She has a wondrous work of God to ponder. And no matter what others may think about this strange manifestation, she knows it was from God. God has a history of doing things for us, through us and *to* us. Often it's the things He does *to us* that leave us pondering.

He knows the ways that I take. When he has tried me, I shall come out like gold. Job 23:10

I love Bill Johnsons teaching on the Immaculate Conception in His series "Revival, The Cost". He rightly highlights how the Virgin Mary treasured the words that the angel spoke to her. She pondered those things in her heart, and from that place of rested submission, God's will was performed in and through her—at a great cost to her. She had to live with the stigma of becoming pregnant out of wedlock. There was no possible way she could have fully understood enough of the angel's request to accept it with any level of *doctrinal* certainty. The important thing was that she yielded to it.

She continued to ponder the entire situation even after she had baby Jesus. [6]

The apostle Paul called himself a "Hebrew of Hebrews" and he was a leader in the Jewish community. Almost overnight, he was hated and eventually hunted by his own peers. Not because he intentionally set out to upset them or because he came to a personal revelation of Jesus after much study and prayer, but because of an out-of-the-box God experience on the road to Damascus. If you read Paul's many letters to the church it is obvious that he pondered his Damascus road encounter frequently.

The *pondering mode* will be almost perpetual for the rest of your life. Not because you are stuck or resistant to the Lord's ways, but because from here on out, you will be constantly challenged with new facets of God's mysterious ways. Especially when dramatic life altering experiences happen to you that are legitimate God encounters. Once the Lord has succeeded at shaking you loose from the religious spirit of comfort-zone Christianity, in His infinite wisdom, He will keep you moving forward. You will constantly be letting go of the present to grab on to the future. Revelation of God's Word will increase as the Lord sets before you other strange and fascinating attributes of Himself, like further mountainous terrains. Once again you will listen, treasure, and ponder from your new vantage point. And once

---

[6] Luke 2:19

again, His Word will unfold in a new and fascinating way. Certain verses that previously meant one thing, now, simultaneously mean another.

When I lived in Idaho, I enjoyed deer hunting. One of the things I discovered on my hunting journeys is that I would become obsessed with scaling whatever mountain or hill lay before me. Our hunting group would set out early in the morning at the base of some hill in the beautiful Sawtooth National Forrest, climbing and traversing to higher ground. By sun-up, we would be perched below a peak with our binoculars gazing off into the vast, open hillsides of Idaho. I loved that feeling of having reached a vantage point, but without fail—as we reached the crown of whatever ridge we were scaling—we would discover that more and higher hills lay ahead. But I always enjoyed the moment, of remaining in one place to ponder our next move. And it was often in the place of stillness that we would spot our game. This is a crude comparison to the spiritual journey, but in a way it does apply. The constant second-guessing, fear-of-risk, doubt and over-dependence on so-called doctrinal purity is spiritually polarizing. But since you have been freed of that mindset, you will begin to experience an ever-ascending Christian lifestyle. God does not mind if you experiment in the realm of the spirit, nor does He mind if you re-examine Scripture in light of your experience. You can now operate from a higher vantage point, knowing that the Lord will set a course for you. And there will be options. The Lord's will for you is not rigid, nor is it cast in stone. He is working in and

through and *with* you. He wants your input. Remember: you have the keys and He trusts you.

Therefore prepare your minds for action, be sober, and set your hope fully on the grace that will be brought to you at the revelation of Jesus Christ. 1 Peter 1:13

The pondering mode is a high and lofty place. It is the mountain peak of freedom. It has the advantage of past experience and the comfort of knowing that what is happening to you is God's doing, not yours. The Lord Himself has set you on this journey because in the secret place you cried out to Him and asked Him to be more real in your life. Rigid "churchianity" and confining doctrines mixed with the undercurrent of skepticism toward any claims of the miraculous were killing you softly... and you've had enough! For some of you, it has come to the unfortunate place that, either God shows up and the power of His Word is available now, or you are done with Christianity!

You have sat idly by long enough. Too many friends and family members have been taken out by sickness and death. You've watched too many young people fall prey to demonic deception as their lives were destroyed or lost. Even many of your Christian friends are falling by the wayside. Marriages are crumbling, and businesses are failing. How long can a person who is filled with the Spirit of a living God accept defeat? Not that you haven't experienced any victories through prayer and God's intervention. But let's face it, there are way too many casualties for a people whose God said *if you ask anything in My Name I will do it.* Does any of this sound familiar, or am I leaking out some of my own journey?

8. To Be Or Not To Be

To be or not to be: That is the question: Whether 'tis nobler in the mind to suffer the slings and arrows of outrageous fortune, or to take arms against a sea of troubles, and by opposing end them. William Shakespeare

The combination of pondering and heavens favor creates a unique season in our Christian experience that will ultimately be perpetual. Another level of embracing mystery is now required. The mystery is, where do you go from here? Like Hamlet you wonder: am I best suited to take the hits that come with great favor, or do I press headlong into embattled territory and bring down anything that opposes God? Along with this new level of mystery comes a new level of freedom and responsibility. This vantage point presents very unordinary options, but praise God you have become tuned to His voice, you embrace the mystery of His ways, and you have learned to rest as you treasure and ponder the testimonies of His works. *It is from this realm and vantage point that cities are taken and nations are saved.*

I personally believe that the Lord is intricately coordinating the culmination of His plan. Most of the detail and prophetic checkpoints are laid out in scripture, but God in His wisdom has also factored into the equation that we the Church are to play an active roll in bringing about God's will on-earth-as-it-is-in-heaven *before* the "day" of the Lord. This active role on our part requires a demonstration of His power. Jesus' ministry on earth was a model of what normal Christianity will look like when He returns. To borrow from New Testament parable language, the landowner wants to return to a generation of productive stewards. Jesus once asked a simple question that is within our power to decide the outcome.

When the Son of Man comes, will he find faith on the earth? Luke 18:8

And the answer is yes, although for now this is where the greater body of Christ is lacking. And I count myself as a contributor to some of that lack. But I am rapidly changing as my hunger for more of God drives me forward. It's one thing to evangelize an unreached people group—a good thing, I might add. It's another to transform our own cities. And *both* are mandated. And this cannot be done without miracles and supernatural intervention. In summary, there is no way to achieve the will of God without demonstrations of the power of God. And whatever vantage point of breakthrough we view the future from, we can rest assured the next hill is higher. The pondering mode is where faith is generated, fostered and maintained. We must intentionally and consciously place value on the process and refuse to let offence and doubt rob from us what we know God has done. "To be or not to be; That is the question."

9. Me And My Angel(s)

One dynamic of the supernatural lifestyle is the actual interaction with the spirit realm. To live a life of miracles, visions, signs and wonders and have acceleration in the gifts of the Holy Spirit we have to learn how to function in the spirit realm. This means opening yourself up to the spirit realm and staying very close to the word of God. If you encounter evil you use the word of God as your defense just like Jesus did.[7] When you encounter the Lord there is no defense needed. You can relax and converse as much as the incident allows.

In the entire course of my life I have visibly seen demons twice. On one occasion the spirit spoke to me in satanic tongues and I knew exactly what it was saying. It was floor to ceiling tall and stood over me in the form of a dark image pointing its finger in my face. It told me that the bible was full of lies. I rebuked it in the name of Jesus and it left the room instantly. The other time I visibly saw a demon is written about with detail in the following chapter.

I have also had three personal face-to-face encounters with Jesus, two of which are described in detail in the next two chapters. And on two occasions I have had visitations from angels of the Lord. One of them is

---

[7] Matthew 4:1-11

described on the back cover of this book. The other is the centerpiece of this chapter. The Jesus encounters were different from all other spiritual encounters because of the amount of time they lasted, the specificity of the conversations, and the sheer intensity of atmosphere, including the effects on my body. In my experience angels are busy and on the go but Jesus likes to take his time and converse.

If anyone hears my voice and opens the door, then I will come in to him, and will dine with him, and he with me. Revelation 3:20

Over the past few years especially, the Holy Spirit established a pattern in our relationship. He will often speak to me in the early hours of the morning just before I am fully awake, usually around 5 a.m. The voice is always the same, and the phrases are very short. Sometimes He will plant images in my mind or instantly grant me solutions to particular dilemmas I may be facing at the time. Most often He will speak one or two words audibly. And I will instantly know what He is referring to. I am reminded of the story of Samuel the Prophet when he was boy living and sleeping in the temple.

Samuel went and lay down in his place. Yahweh came, and stood, and called as at other times, "Samuel! Samuel!" Then Samuel said, "Speak; for your servant hears." 1 Samuel 3:910

One morning in 2013 I was half awake, and I could hear a conversation in the corner of the room near the door that leads out to our deck. At first I thought it was the Lord but quickly realized there was more than one voice in the room and I knew it wasn't Jesus nor was it demonic. I tried to intentionally awaken myself completely but I was unable to open my eyes. I was being held in my current state of consciousness not able to move or open my eyes. There was no fear whatsoever in the room as I lay there and listened. Three angels were having a casual conversation about who their favorite worship leaders in our church were. One of the angels was presenting a strong case on behalf of one particular female singer, and after some light and humorous debate, they all agreed. It was so random and seemingly unimportant dialogue, but I am honored that they felt comfortable in my home as I just lay there listening. It was like listening to casual lunch-break conversation on one of the hundreds of construction sites I have worked on, pleasant, light-hearted and humorous.

What I love about this story is that I have come to a place where I don't have to know why the angels let me listen in on their conversation. I just love the fact, and I do say fact, that these angels were casually socializing in my bedroom. When you think about it, it is biblically consistent that at 5 a.m. ministering guardian angels would be having some leisure time while *their assignments* were sleeping. I would like to think that at least one of those is my guardian angel. Although, looking back at my life, it might be all three?

One hallmark of this encounter was that I was instantly able to tell the difference between a voice of an angel and the voice of my Lord, and that I understood them. Were they speaking English? Or was I interpreting the tongues of angels.

If I speak with the languages of men and of angels...
1st Corinthians 13:1

In the course of my life I have heard the voice of angels, the voice of demons and the voice of the Lord. I know the difference.

My sheep hear my voice, and I know them and they follow me. John 10:27

The Apostle Paul spoke often of angels and had visitations from them....

For there stood by me this night an angel, belonging to the God whose I am and whom I serve, saying, 'Don't be afraid, Paul. You must stand before Caesar. Behold, God has granted you all those who sail with you. Acts 27:23-24

Based on Paul's writings he obviously assumed that Gods people would occasionally interact with angels too...

But even though we, or an angel from heaven, should preach to you any "good news" other than that which we preached to you, let him be cursed. Galatians 1:8

It is important that we learn to discern the voices spoken from the spirit realm, recognize angelic visitations and the demonic. It is called *"discerning spirits"*. [8] History is laced with men and women who have interacted with demons claiming they were interacting with angels of the Lord and have developed dangerous doctrines. And some of these doctrines are adversely affecting the world today.

For such men are false apostles, deceitful workers, masquerading as Christ's apostles. And no wonder, for even Satan masquerades as an angel of light. It is no great thing therefore if his servants also masquerade as servants of righteousness, whose end will be according to their works. 2 Corinthians 11:13-15

Because of this many within the church have thrown the baby out with the bath water by steering those under their leadership away from supernatural activity altogether. Instead they delve deep into the bible in an effort to become intellectually superior. The unintended consequence of biblical intellectual superiority (so called) is supernatural inferiority. This is not wise and leads to what I call one legged Christianity, able to hop along the right path with the security of their biblical crutch, but never able to run.

Christianity is a supernatural lifestyle therefore we must learn to function accordingly.

---

[8] 1 Corinthians 12:10

10. Love To Be Loved

The Tuesday regional leaders meeting at Bethel was off to a great start. There were at least 40 people in the room, and the stories of miracles and testimonies of people getting saved and set free from all kinds of maladies were flowing. I was still new to the Bethel revival culture and had yet to have any dramatic events like the ones I heard about at the meeting. But lingering in my mind was a bizarre event that had taken place in my bedroom two nights prior.

As I lay sleeping, a demonic spirit began pouncing on me and choking me, and something held my arms to my sides. I fought to break free to no avail. The breath had been taken from my lungs, and my ability to call on the name of Jesus was stifled. The commotion woke my wife Doreen. She could hear me gasping as I tried to speak the name of Jesus. The air around me had turned freezing cold. My wife could actually reach her hand into the icy air and pull it back into the warm air. My feet were being elevated as the evil spirit tried to hang me upside down. I was finally able get my right arm free and push through the upper left torso of the demonic spirit. I could see its whole shoulder section light up in blue as my hand passed through him. My tongue was suddenly loosed, and I rebuked the spirit in the Name of Jesus. Instantly, it left the room. This sobering encounter circulated in my mind as I sat in the Tuesday meeting. I wasn't about to share this story; it would have been like throwing a pale of cold water on everyone.

The meeting broke out into an intense prayer and prophecy time. The room grew electric with the power of God's presence. A gentleman named Ernest Roberts was prophesying over a couple of pastors from central California who said they were considering quitting the ministry. Earnest spoke with power and authority into their situation, and we all watched as these men dropped back into their chairs with hands lifted as they received the words and prayers spoken over them. Many other people had chimed in, and the entire group was focused on restoring these broken servants. I stood on the perimeter looking on. Then *that voice* spoke. That voice that comes from *that certain place* and touches *that certain place* of my consciousness. The voice of God said, "Ask Ernest to pray for you."

I had not yet formally met Earnest. He was now standing near me, and I said to him: "The Lord is telling me to ask you to pray for me." Ernest smiled real big and said "sure."

As I bowed my head and turned my palms toward the sky, Earnest said, "I am going to punch you in the stomach."

I responded, "No you're not!"

Too late! Earnest had thrust his fist toward my stomach, stopping just shy of actually hitting me.

Then he stepped back and looked at me with expectation. I responded again, "I am not falling down." Suddenly, as if there was a hand on my chest and a hand on my back, I was being laid down by an invisible force. It was like an invisible man was baptizing me. I grabbed for Earnest shirt, but he pulled back out of my reach. I could not resist the power that held me, and down I went, plastered to the ground as if I weighed a thousand pounds. And I could not get up. Then I heard *the voice* again, "It's me and I love you."

"And when I saw him, I fell at his feet dead. And he laid his right hand on me, saying unto me, Fear not..."
Revelation 1:17

I was face to face with God. It was as if Jesus was sitting on me with His face to my face as He held my arms down. Low voltage electricity began to pulse throughout my body, and my entire being trembled lightly as I concentrated on breathing. I was paralyzed on the floor, and tears flowed down the side of my face filling my ears then pouring out of my ears onto the ground. The Lord continued to speak: "It's me and I love you, don't resist."

I said, "I am so sorry Lord, I am so sorry." I am reminded of Daniel's God encounter:

"How can someone like me, your servant, talk to you my lord? My strength is gone, and I can hardly breathe." Then one who looked like a man touched me again, and I felt my strength returning. "Don't be

afraid," he said, "for you are precious to God. Peace! Be encouraged! Be strong!" Daniel 10:17-19

I realized at that moment that I didn't really know the Lord the way I thought I did. I had actually been resistant to the Holy Spirit. The Lord was encouraging me and revealing the truth about our relationship. Then I recalled the event two nights before when the demon was trying to hang me by my feet. There is a drastic difference between the presence of demons and the presence of God.

Right at that moment of realization, a woman named Anne Kalvastrand came and knelt at my feet, holding them to the ground as she prayed. I hadn't told anybody about the demonic visitation, and now there was Anne holding my feet down to the ground as if to say, "I've got you covered."

After about 15-20 minutes I was able to lift myself off the ground. Earnest saw me getting up, and he crossed the room, slapped me on the shoulder, and said, "God is not finished with you yet."

Bam! Down I went again, and the whole process started up once more. This time I was fully surrendered as the power of God literally came through me in waves. From that day on, I began to devour the Word of God. You should see my Bible. The post-encounter parts of it are marked all over the margins and in every gap with all kinds of new insight and revelation. I could preach and teach scripture without having to open the Bible. God's

Word just rolls off my tongue. And miracles are now common occurrences. It's unusual for a day to pass by that the Lord doesn't give me specific things to say to people, often people I don't know, or minister healing to someone. Now the *voice* of God is much more frequent and much clearer.

That particular event was the turning point in my Christian life. I trembled for many days after, and randomly become totally overwhelmed by Gods love. Multiple times a day I would catch myself on the verge of tears, as the old rigid know-it-all Brian was being purged from my soul and spirit. I have moments when I can feel the manifest presence of love come over me. Sometimes this would happen at church and random people who I don't know will sense the love of God and start hugging me. Sometimes 3 or 4 will approach me, all within a couple minutes of each other.

The ultimate baptism of the Holy Spirit is the baptism of love. Above all the gifts of the Holy Spirit the Paul Apostle Paul describes love as the "more excellent way". If there is only one thing you take from this book I hope it is the desire to be overtaken physically, emotionally and spiritually by the love of God.

Blessed are those who hunger and thirst after righteousness, for they shall be filled. Matthew 5:6

Keep yourselves in God's love, looking for the mercy of our Lord Jesus Christ to eternal life. Jude 21

11. Jesus Likes Me, This I Know

It was a typical Monday morning for me. I decided to go to the church office to pay the monthly bills and take care of whatever administrative jobs beckoned. Our little congregation in Redding, California had been generous; we had renovated, and we were all quite proud of our newly decorated sanctuary. We had cantina-style bar tables and chairs for seating, high-tech graphic carpet with a plush, black carpet border around the room, dark burgundy and mustard colored walls with a black ceiling, a cherry-wood floor on the stage, and hanging ball lamps for lighting. The walls were covered with all kinds of art that wasn't typical in a church sanctuary, including large prints of famous events and places in recent church history. One print was of Pirates Cove, Newport Beach in the early 1970's where Chuck Smith was baptizing hundreds of people. Another print was of the old, dilapidated Azusa Street Revival building, another of Billy Graham preaching in the 60's in Trafalgar Square. And my personal favorite was a close up of Lonnie Frisbee baptizing a young girl in the Pacific Ocean.

This little church had become my own personal expression of what I thought a church should look and feel like. Our little congregation loved it. It looked like a sanctified, rustic cantina. If you were to visit us on a Sunday morning, the first thing you would encounter as you walked in the front lobby was a large video monitor rotating short videos. A typical video set might include the famous Laird Hamilton surfing a gargantuan wave at Teahupoo Tahiti with a caption saying, "With God all things are possible." Then the video would fade into a black and white of Johnny Cash with his acoustic guitar singing about the blood of Jesus. That would fade into an interview with leaders of an underground church in Egypt, which faded into Elvis Presley singing How Great Thou Art. The video cycle ended with 1950's footage of Billy Graham preaching, and then would start all over again. The motivation behind the unusual decorating and seemingly unrelated video collage was to disarm the religious spirit. I liked greeting first time visitors with the mix of imagery and ideas. I could almost read their minds as they entered the room: "Azusa Street, Chuck Smith, Billy Graham, Lonnie Frisbee, Johnny Cash, Elvis Presley? What did I get myself into?"

The background, pre-service music playing through the P.A. system was a mix of Christian and secular music. I loved to play secular music that I believed to be the songwriter crying out for God, followed by another song that answered their cry. It wasn't uncommon to hear Social Distortion, Midnight Oil, Johnny Cash, and Brian & Jenn Johnson—in that order. I also liked playing gospel music by Johnny Cash and Elvis Presley and Bob Dylan, and many others who didn't fit the typical church mold of what a Christian spokesperson should look or act like.

My pulpit was made out of heavy wrought iron, and I often preached barefoot. A self-serve debit machine with a card swipe stood in the lobby with a sign over it reading: "Bring your tithes to the storehouse."

You might have guessed I have zero aspirations to fulfill traditional assumptions about how a church should look, act, think, or feel. The entire décor, combined with the music, videos, and artwork was like one of Jesus' parables. A few got it, most didn't. And I loved that. My desire was to build a church of unconditional lovers who would follow their hearts, not their heads.

But on this particular Monday morning, I entered our beautiful little eclectic "church" knowing that in just a few short weeks we were going to close our doors for good. Yes, we had decided to close the church. The congregation did not know it yet because the decision had yet to be made official, but I knew it was the right thing to do, especially after what hadn't happened over the last seven weeks.

Eight weeks prior to this particular Monday, on a Sunday morning as I preached, something came over me. A raw and pure moment of honesty and total transparency was about to burst forth from my lips, and I knew I could not contain it. The dramatic, face-to-face God encounter I described earlier had radically shifted my heart. I was now regularly attending the Bethel Tuesday Regional Leaders Meetings, and I was a different person than the one who originally planted the church—and my congregation knew it. In a sudden, unplanned moment that was as surprising to me as it was to our congregation, I stepped down from the podium platform onto the carpet and said, "I can't do this anymore."

Suddenly, there it was, the most honest sermon I had ever preached. I could see the instant shift on people's faces as eyebrows went up. I poured my heart out like never before and told the church, "If God doesn't show up, I will quit". I decided that for the next seven weeks, I wouldn't preach, and we wouldn't have any worship music. There would only be prayer and intercession. Our little group had no idea what that looked like. And to be honest, neither did I.

Some of the church members eventually asked me, "What are you expecting to happen?" I would tell them, "I don't know, but when and if it does, we will *all* know." I was hoping for the ground to shake and the foundation of the building to crack. Anything! I honestly did not care how the Lord did it, but it had to be Him doing it!

And nothing happened.

Even after seven Sundays in a row of corporate prayer and intercession, there was no evidence of what I hoped for. Others within the fellowship disagreed. But I wasn't after a few tears or a more loving, tight-knit little church. I wasn't after the satisfaction of knowing that after seven weeks of

prayer only there were still tithes in the box. I wasn't after camaraderie or any form of human emotional display or outburst. I was hoping to appeal to the throne of God and persuade Him to come to us. I had really laid it all on the line, and I meant it. I remember after everyone left the church on that final Sunday of prayer, my son-in-law Brandon and I looked at each other with a bit of sadness. He knew me well enough to know I wasn't kidding. We discussed briefly the closing of the church. That was the backdrop of this particular Monday morning, which was the day after the seventh Sunday of prayer.

Another dynamic had been set in motion that Sunday evening, just before I went to bed. I had purchased a book by Benny Hinn titled *Welcome, Holy Spirit*. It was a huge step for me because my ministry affiliation/denomination was (in our typical under-the-radar, innuendo style) opposed to Benny Hinn for his opulent living and what I considered to be a charlatan approach to healing ministry. I even considered him borderline heretic. And now, here I was, reading his book. I was completely overwhelmed by it! I cried multiple times as I flipped from page to page learning for the first time that I could talk to and pray to the person of the Holy Spirit. I felt so ashamed for my judgmental attitude towards Benny Hinn—a man I didn't even know. I realized that I did not know the person of the Holy Spirit. I knew about His gifts and about His work on the earth, but I didn't know Him personally.

As I entered the church that Monday morning, I was carrying a file folder, my laptop computer, my Bible and Benny Hinn's book. It was now exactly fifty days—to the hour—since the day I had stepped down from that pulpit and drove my stake into the ground…. And He came!

When I entered the lobby, the sanctuary doors blew open gently all by themselves. I stopped and curiously looked into the room and felt as though I was being lured in, so I went. The moment I entered the room, I knew it was different. Its as if something was in the air figuratively speaking. I sensed that someone was in the room. And I realized that the "someone" was the manifest glory of God. I sat on the couch and began to weep.

I said, "Holy Spirit, I am so sorry for ignoring you all these years." I began to worship Him and give Him thanks. I was no longer worried that I would somehow offend Jesus or the Father by worshipping the Holy Spirit. All I knew was: it was He, He is a person, and He is God. How that works is for *them* to sort out. Then He, the Holy Spirit introduced me to Him. Jesus stepped into the realm of consumed space where the Holy Spirit stood and was now in the room standing over me. I couldn't visibly see Him with my natural eyes, but I could tell where He stood and could discern His body language. It was as if my natural vision had partnered with my spirit vision, and both were being passed through the filter of my heart. I began to cry more, and He asked me to stop. He pointed to my Bible, so I picked it up and opened

to the text in Luke where I had left off the last time I had last preached:

Now while the multitude pressed on him and heard the word of God, he was standing by the lake of Gennesaret. He saw two boats standing by the lake, but the fishermen had gone out of them, and were washing their nets. He entered into one of the boats, which was Simon's, and asked him to put out a little from the land. He sat down and taught the multitudes from the boat. When he had finished speaking, he said to Simon, "Put out into the deep, and let down your nets for a catch." Simon answered him, "Master, we worked all night, and took nothing; but at your word I will let down the net." When they had done this, they caught a great multitude of fish, and their net was breaking. Luke 5:1-6

After I read the text, the Lord asked me, "Why do you think I blessed Peter with that great catch of fish?" I quickly responded with the common analogy about how Jesus was using the great catch of fish as a metaphor and a teaching tool about effective evangelism.

Jesus asked me again, "Why do you think I blessed Peter with that great catch of fish?" So I rebounded with another typical analogy about the importance of obeying God's voice if we want to be successful.

Then the Lord said, for the third time with emphasis, "Why do *you* think I blessed Peter with that great catch of fish?"

At that moment, I realized that the Lord wasn't interested in what I had learned from others about His word, but rather He was interested in my own personal take on that transaction between Peter and Jesus.

I got up from my chair, walked about twenty feet, turned around, threw my hands in the air, and responded with a bit of consternation mixed with humility: "I don't know why you did that! I have no idea why you blessed Peter with that great catch of fish."

Jesus quickly responded, "Because I like Peter." There was a pause as I felt His eyes that burn like flames of fire piercing into my very soul, and then He said, "I like you too."

(Pause here and encounter Jesus. He wants to meet with you. He likes you, too.)

I can't put into words the warmth and the peace that immediately saturated my entire being. In a moment, I realized that I am a friend of God and that He valued our friendship enough to come to me. It is one thing to know that Jesus *loves me*. But, He *likes me* too? This is empowering and comforting. I lifted my hands and began to worship Him. I started crying again, and the Lord quickly said, "Stop crying."

I said, "I'm trying, I'm trying!" as I wiped my hands across my face.

His response made perfect sense in that moment. He wanted to hang out and have a conversation, not stand there and watch me cry. Just like any other friend who wants to make use of our time together. Then He went on to tell me how much the boat meant to Peter. Peter was a fisherman, and the boat was his livelihood, and because Peter allowed the Lord to minister from his boat the Lord decided to bless Peter back. I understand that what I am writing here is not in the Bible, but if I were to withhold the details of this time spent with Jesus, it would be the same as editing what He had told me. So I must relay the whole story.

At this point, I was standing about twenty feet from where the presence of the Lord rested, and my back was to the main door from the sanctuary to the lobby. For whatever reason, I thought our conversation was over. I was still in a state of bliss realizing that I was a personal friend of the Lord. I felt like the apostle John who referred to himself as the "one whom Jesus loved."

I turned to the doors and started to exit the room, but the Lord spoke again, asking: "Where are you going? I quickly spun around and said, "I don't know. I don't know where to go from here. I have no idea what to do or what to say."

Then the Lord said, "From now on, I want you to learn to function in my presence." And then He was gone.

From that day until this, my life has been a whirlwind of God's goodness and abundance. The Lord has paid us back with massive interest for every "boat" we have ever "loaned" Him. Jesus is my Lord, Jesus is my savior, Jesus is my King, and Jesus is my friend!

... and he vanished out of their sight. They said to one another, "Weren't our hearts burning within us, while he spoke to us along the way, and while he opened the Scriptures to us?" - Luke 24:31-32

12. Invitation For Expectation Of Visitation

One of the attributes of God that we so often forget is His desire to be with us. Jesus Christ literally gave up heaven, stepped into this world, and sacrificed His own body unto death to have personal fellowship with us. At this juncture, I want to connect the dots between two seemly-unrelated Bible verses.

He entered and was passing through Jericho. ² There was a man named Zacchaeus. He was a chief tax collector, and he was rich. ³ He was trying to see who Jesus was, and couldn't because of the crowd, because he was short. ⁴ He ran on ahead, and climbed up into a sycamore tree to see him, for he was going to pass that way. ⁵ When Jesus came to the place, he looked up and saw him, and said to him, "Zacchaeus, hurry and come down, for today I must stay at your house." Luke 19:1-5

When we first glance at this story, we have the tendency to place the emphasis on Zacchaeus' noble effort to get a glance of Jesus. I am personally more intrigued with how easily Jesus was impressed. Zacchaeus might have done the same thing (and probably did) for any entourage coming into town that caused a small stir. It would be safe to assume that because Zacchaeus was a short man he scaled the tree often. The beauty of this story is how easily and readily Jesus invited himself to dine with Zacchaeus. Jesus pursued friendship with Zacchaeus. Is it possible that Zacchaeus had a genuine desire to host the presence of Jesus in His home that exceeded the desire of everyone else? Which leads me to this next verse:

Behold, I stand at the door and knock. If anyone hears my voice and opens the door, then I will come in to him, and will dine with him, and he with me. Revelation 3:20

The context of this verse from Revelation is important. We often quote it when encouraging someone to give his or her life to Jesus. It is one of the top-ten, all-time, come-to-Jesus quotes. But! That is not what this verse is about. The *resurrected* Jesus made this statement after He ascended into heaven. The apostle John was having an encounter with the resurrected Christ on the Isle of Patmos. The statement is directed at the already believing church. Jesus is promising to come and have personal fellowship *with any person who hears His voice and opens the door.*

Remember the first chapter of this book? The supernatural lifestyle begins when we can hear the voice of God: when we become voice activated. And for any person who can hear His voice, Jesus is promising a personal visit for those who are willing just like He had with Zacchaeus.

Not long ago I set up a healing tent at a very large Christian music festival. My team and I spent two, entire days—from mid morning until dusk—laying hands on the sick and praying with and for people. It was a great time, and God performed some wondrous miracles. Unfortunately, trying to minister healing at a Christian festival isn't embraced the way you might think it should be. A large scale Christian gathering of multiple denominations and beliefs tends be generally skeptical of healing ministries. The final eve of this event closed with a famous and internationally known Christian band. I love their songs, and they played a fantastic set. As the evening drew to a close, the lead singer of the band started preaching. My heart sank as he used his platform to eloquently vent his opinion against the idea that Christians should expect more of God and more of the Holy Spirit than what they received on their day of salvation. He emphasized the completeness of salvation, but he went way overboard.

This highly influential, famous singer stood in front of a crowd of at least five thousand and said, "The next time your pastor says, 'who wants more of the Holy Spirit?' raise your hand and tell him that there isn't any more because when you asked Jesus to come into your heart, all the fullness of God and His Holy Spirit came in.'" Then he quoted a couple of Bible verses to prove his position. I honestly don't think the general audience had any idea of the size of the horse-pill they were being asked to swallow because of the high profile of this person, his persuasive style, and his meticulous quoting of Bible verses that made it all sound so right.

What this singing preacher fails to realize is that the Bible is filled with absolute truths that oppose each other. Yes, when we received Jesus Christ as Lord, the fullness of God entered us, but it is equally as true that there is more of God's fullness, anointing, and power available to us. One of the reasons we know there is more—a greater measure of God's power and presence—is because those who are brave enough to ask for it with sincerity and consistency get it. Why would Jesus knock on the door of the church hoping to be let in? Not because He wants to get to know you better but rather *He wants to be known by you better.* He offered more of His presence to the church of Laodicea than they already had.

It is sermons like the singer's that keep Christians sealed in defeat. That audience was robbed of their ability to hope and dream of greater and more significant encounters with their God and instead was forced to look inside themselves for what was missing—thus being set-up for condemnation. And yet the entire plan of God's redemption is for the purpose of restoring fellowship between God and man. And I am appalled that so much of Christianity readily puts off until heaven those things that we can have now. And intimate encounters with Jesus are one of those things; Even personal visitations. Referring to a post ascension encounter of his own the Apostle Paul said, *"Have I not seen Jesus our Lord?".* [9]

---

[9] 1st Corinthians 9:1

It is in the pursuit of Him, His presence, His anointing, and His power that your personal destiny is fulfilled and His will is accomplished here on earth as it is in heaven. I don't care who you are or what your history with God is, you can have more of Him. And in the supernatural lifestyle expectation is everything. After Jesus rose from the dead the disciples of Jesus literally hung out with Him face to face. They ate with Him, camped with Him, and listened to Him teach them. And they discovered in Acts 2 that there was still *more.*

As you read the following excerpt from the Book of Ephesians, notice that the premise is the church's dis-unity of faith and lack of the knowledge of God's Son. And to remedy this, the Lord ordained leaders in various offices within the church to help bring God's people into a greater maturity concerning God's Son Jesus Christ:

He gave some to be apostles; and some, prophets; and some, evangelists; and some, shepherds and teachers; For the perfecting of the saints, to the work of serving, to the building up of the body of Christ; until we all attain to the unity of the faith, <u>and of the knowledge of the Son of God</u>, to a full grown man, to the measure of the stature of the fullness of Christ; Ephesians 4:11-13

The point here is to encourage you to pursue a greater revelation of the person of Jesus Christ. And there is no better way for that to happen than for Jesus to visit you and talk with you like a friend. Throughout Scripture, we read that He visited Daniel and the apostle Paul, Peter, John, and many others. And throughout history, we have heard thousands of testimonies of people—including small children—having personal encounters with Jesus. He appeared supernaturally and walked for seven miles on the road to Emmaus with two of His followers, teaching them from the *"writings of Moses and all the prophets, explaining from all the scriptures the things concerning Himself."* [10] Don't you want those kinds of moments with your Lord and friend? Many people have been robbed of that expectation, but I hope you will reclaim it. There is so much more that Jesus wants to tell you.

In Proverbs 8 Solomon wrote about what I believe to be Jesus manifesting in the form of divine wisdom giving glory and honor and *inspiration* to the Father in the creation process. The phrase "brought forth" in the following text is derived from the single Hebrew verb *khul.* Its primary meaning is to "twist and whirl and dance about" [11]

I was set up from everlasting, from the beginning, before the earth existed. When there were no depths, I was brought forth, when there were no springs abounding with water. Before the mountains were settled in place, before the hills, I was brought forth; while as yet he had not made the earth, nor the fields, nor the beginning of the dust of the world. When he

---

[10] Luke 24

[11] Strong's Concordance H2342

established the heavens, I was there; when he set a circle on the surface of the deep, when he established the clouds above, when the springs of the deep became strong, when he gave to the sea its boundary, that the waters should not violate his commandment, when he marked out the foundations of the earth; then I was the craftsman by his side. I was a delight day by day, always rejoicing before him, Rejoicing in his whole world. My delight was with the sons of men - Proverbs 8:23-31.

Proverbs 8 offers a unique view into the pre-incarnate world of Jesus Christ. If you read "wisdom" here as Jesus, like I do, you see Him dancing and spinning in the splendor and the glory of God the Father in heaven's eternal realm. As if to provide inspiration in the creation process, Jesus is "brought forth," and in His twirling, swirling, spinning, dancing presence the universe is created in all its beauty. Then humanity is created in the image of God/Jesus, and Jesus says, "My delight was with the sons of men."

It is the recognition of God's desire to be with you that will embolden you to invite Him to come to you. Once we are convinced He is available then the ball is in our court. Jesus proved in the Zacchaeus story that He is easily drawn to personal fellowship. And He tells us in Revelation 3:20 that He even "stands at the door and knocks".

Ask the Lord to come to you and visit you like a friend. He will come because He has been waiting for this moment all your life. Many of you have had these kinds of experiences with Jesus already and you want more.

We must ask the Lord to grace us with a hunger for Him that literally draws on His already proven will and desire to be with us. Invite Him and He will come. Or get to a vantage point where you can see Him and He will invite Himself.

"If a man loves me, he will keep my word. My Father will love him, and we will come to him, and make our home with him. John 14:23

13. Resurrection Eschatology

I cannot think of a more controversial subject in the church today than the study of eschatology. Eschatology is the study of end times and many if not most of our contemporary views of it are usually negative. Let me start off by saying that all eschatological interpretations—including mine—are based on a certain level of speculation, emotion and assumptions. I am more interested in the attitude and fruit of a particular eschatology than I am in the actual theory and interpretation of the eschatology itself. After all, we the Church will be forever fine-tuning our eschatology's until the actual day of the Lord.

For the supernatural Christian to live with any degree of consistency and success in the realm of signs, wonders, miracles, and prophetic influence, we must live within a constant state of hope for a better future.

When Isaiah prophesied the coming of Jesus Christ into the world, he described it this way:

For to us a child is born. To us a son is given; and the government will be on his shoulders. His name will be called Wonderful, Counselor, Mighty God, Everlasting Father, Prince of Peace. Of the increase of his government and of peace there shall be no end, on David's throne, and on his kingdom, to establish it, and to uphold it with justice and with righteousness from that time on, even forever. The zeal of Yahweh of Armies will perform this. Isaiah 9:6-7

This pre-introduction of the birth of Jesus Christ describes an ever-increasing government of peace that is guaranteed by the "zeal of Yahweh". That is a strong guarantee. That and Jesus' entire mission to save and reconcile everything He created is the grid through which we should view the future. Based on these precepts our prophetic beliefs and declarations should be founded on this promise of God.

One of the more confusing phrases in the New Testament is "last days" or "final days." Those words seem so non-objective, general, and ambiguous. The author of the book of Hebrews wrote:

God who at various times and in various ways spoke in time past to the fathers by the prophets has in these last days spoken to us by His Son. Hebrews 1-1

It is important to understand the Jewishness of this New Testament book. It is written to the Hebrews, and the ancestors and prophets referred to are Jews. And the case in point is that Jesus, God's Son, is the "last days" sign for the Jews. Notice that the author of Hebrews does not explain his own last days' position but rather assumes it. This begs the question: why?

Prior to raising Lazarus from the dead, Jesus has a conversation with Lazarus' sister, Martha:

Therefore Martha said to Jesus, "Lord, if you would have been here, my brother wouldn't have died. ²² Even now I know that, whatever you ask of God, God will give you." Jesus said to her, "Your brother will rise again." Martha said to him, "I know that he will rise again in the resurrection at the last day." Jesus said to her, "I am the resurrection and the life. He who believes in me will still live, even if he dies. Whoever lives and believes in me will never die. Do you believe this?" John 11:21-25

What I want to point out here is that Martha's belief was that the resurrection of the dead Jesus referred to would be a grand resurrection on *the* "last day." From that conversation with Martha, Jesus goes on to raise Lazarus from the dead, thus proving that the resurrection Martha hoped for was held, contained, and manifest in the *person* of Jesus Christ. And, as we all know, Jesus Himself rose from the dead. And when He rose, so did many others. How awesome is that?

The graves were opened; and many bodies of the saints who had fallen asleep arose: and coming out of the tombs after his resurrection, they entered into the holy city and appeared to many. Matthew 27:52

How does this dynamic transfer into the present? Is it possible that when the New Testament authors say "last days," they are writing from a pretext that is founded in their Jewish eschatology that assumes when the dead begin to rise they are in the last days?

Therefore in their minds resurrection power was the premier sign of the times.

When Jesus was asked to prove Himself with a sign, He pointed to His soon-to-be-realized resurrection:

Then certain of the scribes and Pharisees answered, "Teacher, we want to see a sign from you." But he answered them, "An evil and adulterous generation seeks after a sign, but no sign will be given to it but the sign of Jonah the prophet. For as Jonah was three days and three nights in the belly of the whale, so will the Son of Man be three days and three nights in the heart of the earth. Matthew 12:38-40

The Jews therefore answered him, "What sign do you show us, seeing that you do these things?" Jesus answered them, "Destroy this temple, and in three days I will raise it up." The Jews therefore said, "It took forty-six years to build this temple! Will you raise it up in three days?" But he spoke of the temple of his body. John 2:18-20

Could it be that the ultimate sign of the times from an historical and contemporary biblical perspective is the resurrection of the dead, and Jesus Christ was the "first-fruits" of this phenomenon? Is it possible that when we see an exponential increase in the miraculous—including dead-raising in the Name of Jesus—then this will be a more accurate barometer of where we may or may not be in the grand, end-time scenario? Unfortunately, so many so-called "last days" experts in our time have made the devil out to

be more powerful than the Church. I recently heard a very famous American pastor say that the Church's primary method of last-days victory will be in the form of martyrdom. That sounds more like Islam to me. He went on to say that there will be an increase in the miraculous but his emphasis was definitely on the suffering of the church as the "antichrist" rises to global domination. He went on to say that the antichrist would deceive "several" billion into the mark of the beast. He is basically casting the Church into the great tribulation as martyrs, then saying to his audience, "Go get 'em!" I don't know about you, but that line of thinking doesn't exactly motivate me.

There are approximately seven billion people on the earth now. This pastor assumes "several billion" will follow Satan's lead in the last days. Does this mean that over half the world is going to fall prey to Satan's pseudo empire? I certainly hope not. When I gave my life to Jesus, I assumed I joined the winning team. If those speculations are accurate, then Jesus better return right now and cut His losses.

I don't believe that's what we're dealing with. My personal position is that several kings or regimes of the earth may align themselves with Satan, but the majority of the human race itself will not. While a political and religious spirit may motivate the rulers of this world, the *people* of this world will reject their ploys and turn to Christ in mass quantities. Satan may succeed at manipulating many of the "kings" of the earth, but not the people. For example, North Korea could be labeled as an evil, satanically controlled government. But! I seriously doubt that regime is representative of the heart and the will of its people. The mistake most eschatology teachers make is in failing to differentiate people from their government.

I also believe that the often-prophesied "billion soul harvest" is a low number. Think about this: if a move of God's Spirit is so powerful as to attract a billion people, it might as well be five or six billion. The momentum of a billion people into the kingdom of heaven will be too irresistible to the rest of humanity. Once the proverbial walls come crashing down on one continent, the rest of the world will follow. All of humanity is hungry for Jesus, not just a certain region. Let's keep in mind that our King is Jesus Christ, the champion of the world, creator of all things, and victor over death itself. In the end, Jesus will be the people's choice.

The Lord told Abraham: *"In thee shall all the families of the earth be blessed"*. [12]

The word "blessed" used in that statement is the Hebrew word *barak*.[13] It means "to kneel or cause to kneel." To not consider the possibility that one day the vast majority of the earth will embrace Jesus as Lord is a form of unbelief.

For all of these reasons, I believe the resurrection power of Jesus Christ manifest in this world could be

[12] Genesis 12:3

[13] Strongs Concordance H1288

the premier sign of the times. Not the rise and increase of Satan's kingdom and slaughter of the Church as some insist.

Satan will kick and scream and throw a fit because he is being defeated, just like some of his demons do when they are being cast out. But the overwhelming tide of global influence will respond to the rising tide God's manifest presence.

So, when the New Testament authors use the phrase "last days" it could be that there is an assumption that goes along with it. The assumption being... when the dead begin to rise.

To put it simply: if you want to expedite the coming of Jesus, then heal the sick, cast out demons, and raise the dead. Literally destroying the works of the devil will culminate in the Church's shared victory over the sting of death, which will be the grand finale of human redemption. The Lord Jesus Himself paved the way to our victory over death with His resurrection, but He has determined that we, who are His representative body on this earth and who are filled with His Holy Spirit, are to bash in the gates of hell, bind the strong man, and plunder his kingdom. The very creations of God whom Satan sought to be worshipped by are the ones who do the plundering. We play an active role, not a passive one, in the end time scenario. And dead raising may be the premier sign of the times.

As I write this chapter in January of 2014, there is a promotional campaign on television and in the theaters across America announcing the spring release of a television series called *Resurrection: Imagine The Impossible.* Even Hollywood is hoping for the impossible.

Maybe we aren't waiting on the return of Jesus but rather He is waiting on the Church to claim our victory based on His resurrection. We're not creating our salvation but rather walking in resurrection power that our salvation provides.

For those of us that adhere to an eschatology that believes in the possibility of an end time rapture this idea I propose should come as no surprise. The rapture itself is a mass resurrection of the dead. The Apostle Paul said

The dead in Christ will rise first, then we who are alive, who are left, will be caught up together with them in the clouds, to meet the Lord in the air. 1st Thessalonians 4:16-1

If we are motivated to live a supernatural lifestyle that includes signs, wonders, and miracles, then we must maintain hope and take heed of how we hear and internalize the word of God. We must be careful not to succumb to the tendency to view the future with sensationalism and fear—and/or the tendency to rely on worn-out eschatological views that have been laced with history of error and often totally misrepresent the heart and the goodness of God. Its time to review the Word of God and—through the lens of "all things are possible" and "God is good"—

even re-examine Bible translations in light of the original Greek and Hebrew to see if we missed something.

In the next section, I'll give you an example of what I mean.

14. Good God Theology

With God's goodness as our lens let's examine one of the more dramatic last days' statements that is so often understood to mean the total annihilation of the earth. I want to challenge the face value interpretation of this text because translators may have missed the thrust and depth of what the Holy Spirit meant to say:

But the day of the Lord will come as a thief in the night; in which the heavens will pass away with a great noise, and the elements will be dissolved with fervent heat, and the earth and the works that are in it will be burned up. 2 Peter 3:10

This sounds pretty drastic. Does it mean that the ever-increasing government of peace mentioned in Isaiah 9:6-7 hasn't started yet? Or will the Lord destroy the earth that we have worked so hard to save and improve? Are we currently participants in the government of God, or are we simply evangelists encouraging people to repent so they can join us in a future, new world after this world is destroyed?

Let me put it another way: was Jesus' resurrection only to prove who He is, or was it also to empower us into becoming who we are? The easy way out of this conundrum would be to give a typical Christian-ese response like: "God's ways are not our ways, after all…who can know the mind of God?" That would be the safe response.

But what if the government Isaiah described began the day Jesus was born? Isaiah seems to connect the starting point of Christ's ever-increasing kingdom to His earthly birth. This is what the Magi who visited the toddler Jesus believed. They actually stirred King Herod's heart to jealousy by admitting that it wasn't Herod they came to see. If you and I want to go down in history as *wise men* then we should look beyond the kingdoms of this present world and learn to become active recipients-of and participants-in the ever-increasing government of God that is established in resurrection power. This adjustment in our mindset opens us up to the realm of increase and peace, which is the same realm where miracles abound. The goodness of God must be our primary lens of Bible interpretation and eschatology. This one adjustment helps us navigate Bible verses like one in 2 Peter with a pre-mindset that is close to the heart of God.

Now lets examine 2 Peter 3:10 with our eyes looking through the lens of Gods goodness and see if we can notice anything different. I want to challenge the popular interpretation of Peter's amazing prophecy. Specifically, the statement: "the elements will be destroyed with intense heat, and the earth and its works will be burned up." This is hard to reconcile with the explicit message of the Gospel, which is supposed to be good news.

Peter's text seems to imply a total meltdown of the earth. Or does it?

The phrase "elements destroyed with intense heat" in its original Greek language is *Stoicheion lyō kausoō.* [14]

Stoichheion: any first thing, from which the others belonging to some series or composite whole take their rise, an element, first principal

Lyo: to loose one bound, i.e. to unbind, release from bonds, set free

Kausoo: to burn up, set fire to.

To me, these definitions lean more toward the liberation of first things and the letting go of that which the Lord no longer wants to exist than it does toward complete destruction. The Bible tells us that everything exists by, for, and through Jesus Christ. The part that our translators may find confusing is the fire. They have assumed that the fire of God is indiscriminately destructive. It is not; it is surgically precise and supernaturally directed at only that which is evil. I have laid hands on many, many people who have asked for healing, only to discover that as the power of God began to restore their infirmity, they would experience a burning sensation at the same time. Some would describe an "intense heat" on the part of the body that was sick. Their

---

[14] Strongs Concordance G4747, G3089, G2741

sickness was being "destroyed with intense heat," and it was a good thing.

I have re-interpreted Peter's prophecy like this: on the "day of the Lord," prison doors are melted away, demonic strongholds are fiercely cast out, and every system of man that oppresses humanity is literally melted and disintegrated. At the same time, everything that is meant to remain is liberated and upheld by the power of His Word according to His promises.

Peter is describing an instantaneous, universal, laser-precise release off all that has been taken captive and a literal, molecular breakdown of all that opposes God. That's not a complete meltdown of the entire earth as some suppose. Instead, it is an instantaneous act of divine justice making all things right. Just like a healing miracle.

This interpretation of 2 Peter 3:10 is one example of why it is important that we learn to view Scripture through the lens of God's goodness and His supernatural power to heal and redeem. A miraculous lifestyle will change the way we view Scripture.

This redemptive idea is enforced as we look further into Peter's prophecy. The phrase *"and the earth and its works will be burned up,"* in its original Greek, according to Strongs Concordance is *ge kai ergon katakaio.*

Ge: the earth, the ground, the inhabited part of the world

Kai: including

Ergon: business, employment, enterprise. This includes craftsmanship and art.

Katakaio: burned up, utterly consumed

Notice that the emphasis is on the enterprise and places of employment. Considering the totality of the text and the overarching theme that Jesus Christ comes to set captives free and to destroy the works of the devil, Peter's prophecy appears to be a very precise and specific purging of the morally deprived enterprises, craftsmanship and art of corrupt human governments and corporations that are scattered across the land, as well as the release of all who are bound and made captives of this system.

Can you imagine the office building of a Christian humanitarian corporation being burned to the ground at the return of Jesus Christ? I don't think so. Revelation 11:18 says specifically that the Lord is going to *"destroy them which destroy the earth."*

In the very next sentence, Peter says,

Therefore since all these things will be destroyed like this, what kind of people ought you to be in holy living and godliness, looking for and earnestly desiring the coming of the day of God, which will cause the burning heavens to be dissolved, and the elements will melt

with fervent heat. But, according to his promise, we look for new heavens and a new earth, in which righteousness dwells. Peter 3:11-13

Twice in this section, the King James translators used the word *dissolved* to replace the Greek word *lyo*. In the previous verse, they used the word *destroyed* to replace *lyo*. Which is it? Remember, *lyo* basically means "to liberate." So in essence, Peter is saying that the church should look keenly for the coming of the Lord because He will liberate everything that has been bound by evil and dissolve all that has evil origin and intent. With this in mind, the coming of the Lord could manifest quite differently than what our sincere and honorable King James translators have described. Jesus' return is not the disintegration of the earth but rather the instant healing of all diseases. It is the deliverance from the demonized and the restoration of all mental maladies and the simultaneous destruction of all that kept them in that state. And it is deliverance for all enterprise, craftsmanship and art that is good and the elimination of all that is bad. Jesus' return is a universal deliverance: The entire planet will be healed, set free, and delivered. That is what we are looking for—the righteous fire of God at His coming.

This following scenario is a bit dramatic, but go with it for a minute. Imagine a Planned Parenthood building on one side of the street and a Crisis Pregnancy Center on the other. At the return of Jesus, the Planned Parenthood facility instantly dissolves. But the people are kept alive, still sitting in

the lobby chairs in the midst of a flattened, dissolved building starring across the street at the fully erect Crisis Pregnancy Center, hearing the sound of the recently aborted babies crying as they instantly return to life as the power of God is released over the entire planet at His return. This is what I believe Peter saw when he said, *"the elements will be destroyed with intense heat, and the earth and its works will be burned up."* The Planned Parenthood institution is of the earth and therefore destroyed. But the Crisis Pregnancy Center is of the Kingdom and thus ever-increasing. This same dynamic will happen all around the world in every sphere of humanity.

"... creation itself also will be delivered from the bondage of decay into the liberty of the glory of the children of God." Romans 8:21

Can you see where I am coming from? We have to examine Scripture in light of the goodness of God and in light of the fact that Jesus saves. This is our primary lens. The supernatural Christian lifestyle demands that we delve into the Word of God with a lens towards hope and restoration. This is where our revelation will come from. Not twisting or contorting out of context but rather examining and re-examining with a heart towards hope. This is not pie-in-the-sky theology. It is the exact opposite. This is boots on the ground with a mind toward destroying the works of the devil. It is time for a new look at Scripture and a reassessing of previous mindsets that have caused us to gaze bleakly towards the future. It is this insistence on the goodness of God and the demand for restitution and reconciliation that sparks our authority to heal sickness, turn back the clock on disease, raise the dead, and command the sea to be still.

As a side-note, I don't think we are the final generation that will usher in the return of Jesus. I explain my position on this in my book, *Heroic Eschatology*. I don't like hearing preachers and evangelists say that we are the" last generation" or that the next harvest of new believers is an end-time harvest, or that Jesus is coming very soon. In my opinion, those phrases can do more harm than good. The insistence on end-times pressure and using that message to motivate people can be borderline manipulation. I don't see how any person on the face of this earth living today could possibly know when Jesus is coming. It is unfortunate that the Church uses end time language to persuade people into the Kingdom, not realizing that the same end time language actually strips the children already in the Kingdom of their ability to hope in a better future. Such an attitude destroys motivation for change, justice, and righteousness. What if our current prophetic message to the world and the church was/is: "The earth shall be full of the knowledge of the Lord as the waters cover the sea" (Isaiah 11:9). Now that's something to get out of bed for!

15. Turn And Face The Strange

Imagine the Lord telling you to take a large clay tile and paint a map of your city on it. Then surround the city with little green army men with tanks and artillery. Now grab your kid's Legos and build a little wall that surrounds the city so no person can escape. Now set up your little half-dome Weber barbeque next to what resembles a sixth-grade class project. Stack a huge pile of cow dung next to the barbeque on one side and over a year's worth of unbaked biscuits and a pallet of water bottles on the other side.

Now that your little scenario is all set up, you can enjoy the pleasure of laying there for a total of 430 days, baking biscuits over a cow dung fire with one arm exposed. And don't even think about turning over because the Lord is going to strap you down. And if you didn't stack up enough cow pie briquettes don't worry; you can burn your own dung.

And so there you are, all tied up next to your toy-soldier village, eating biscuits baked over crap, drinking bottled water, and your neighbor walks in. You quickly respond: "God told me to do this" as they are dialing 911.

Welcome to Ezekiel's world. Or should I say: welcome to the world of an obedient servant of the Lord who is willing to do whatever the Lord asks of them (See Ezekiel 3-4). The world of supernatural

Christianity is a world where strange things happen and people do strange things.

If you want to experience the power of God, be party to miracles, and have a Christian experience that is marked by the miraculous, then you must be willing to overlook behavior that you don't understand. If you want to hang around places where God moves with power, then timid, easily offended Christian attitudes must be left at the door. This is a fact! Don't think for a minute that you can wade yourself into this kind of lifestyle in such a way that allows you to measure how deep you want to go. Either you want to see God move or you don't. And if you do you must be willing to step over the bodies of people who have fallen down under the power of God without judging whether or not they are faking it. You must be willing to pray and worship in rooms filled with people laughing uncontrollably, shaking their heads, and walking around with their heads bobbing and dipping. When the raw power of God is present and swirling around in the room, people do strange things. Not all of them but some of them…and it's OK! You might even develop a twitch yourself.

Unfortunately, much of Christianity has decided that strange behavior in the church or amongst Christians must be evil. The problem with this assumption is that God has proven over and over—not only throughout the Bible but also throughout history—that He could care less about societal social grace and protocol when it comes to the way He accomplishes "on earth as it is in heaven." Heaven itself is full of

bizarre creatures, elaborate ceremonies, and large-scale productions of symbolic prophetic acts.

Imagine: when Jesus walked this earth, God in the form of man was on His best behavior. Do you understand that Jesus was reserved in His behavior? Even though He would stick mud in the eye of a blind man, cast demons into a herd of pigs, and raise the dead right out of their coffins at the city gate— during the actual funeral. He even performed exorcisms right smack in the middle of His own sermon, in church, without skipping a beat. Then he left church to go walk around town healing the sick. I have Christian friends who get offended because I heal people in public places, and the same people have taken offense to my ministry because I minister healing *in church*. I have discovered that when the power of God is present, Christians get nervous but sinners get saved, healed, and delivered. You do the math.

After having had the two major God encounters I've mentioned in this book, my personal ministry took on some *unique nuances*. In the following chapter are accounts of strange behavior and the results that accompanied these unusual and fun acts of God.

16. Harnessing Power

In February of 2013, my wife and I were ministering to a small group of people on the island of Kauai. After a series of house-to-house meetings, we ended up in a local art and dance studio for a grand finale. The word got out that miracles were happening, and the Holy Spirit was giving very accurate words of knowledge that were flowing into powerful, life-altering prophecies.

About thirty people had gathered in this little studio. We had an awesome time of praise and worship. When I got up to preach, I started off with some words of knowledge. I try to start off my sermons with some kind of demonstration that God is working through and in me. I don't remember all that was said, but I do know it was accurate, and God was establishing Himself in the room. It's what happened next that I want to highlight.

After a brief sermon, I went right into a time of healing. Since it was a small crowd, I just asked for anyone to stand who needed a physical healing or a miracle. About six or seven people stood. I asked them all to come up to the front of the room and stand in a line. During this time, the acoustic, island-style worship team started praising again.

I noticed that two people in the room were under a heavy dose of God's presence. One person was shaking and their head was bobbing up and down. The other was moving the same way, with a lot of laughter bursting forth. As I ministered to each person I would interview them while at the same time paying attention to the God-inspired thoughts in my own mind. While I did this, a few of the ladies crowded around to hear and be involved in the ministry time. This made me a little nervous because I was concerned about the privacy of the individual and also wanted to make sure there was some order in the way I ministered. I personally feel it's excessive when multiple people are standing around one person shouting and rebuking and praying, with no one in charge.

In my mind, I saw an image of the two people shaking and laughing and myself holding hands in a chain. So I brought them forward and we held hands. Then I asked the women who had come forward to be involved in the ministry time to lay their hands on my shoulder and pray for me as I ministered. Then I told the two people with whom I was holding hands to shake and laugh all they wanted. When they felt a surge of God's power they were to squeeze my hand, at which point I would release that through my other hand onto the person. You can imagine what this looked like to observers. There I was holding hands with two "charismaniacs" who were shaking and laughing with total passion and abandonment to the Holy Spirit while three women with their hands on my head and shoulders were praying passionately and aggressively as I was laying my hand on the person to be healed who was having their own

encounter with God. We had succeeded in corporately harnessing the power of God, in unity, with the desire to get these people healed.

And it worked!

Boy did it work. The following is an email from Lucinda Teter who stood by me praying: I have removed the names of the rest of the individuals for privacy sake.

Okay Brian, I just received another report of a healing from the time you came here and we hosted a tent meeting at our house and had the mini conference at KUGA... Just got word tonight that _____ back was healed. He was at the mini conference at KUGA and had serious back issues. He told ____ & _____ tonight that he was healed when you were here. We (you and those with you) prayed for him at the end when you also prayed for ____, while ____ and _____ played music. So here is what I know. These people reported healing...

1) Women at my house whose daughter had been killed and she suffered from back pain and grief, that night something lifted off her and she felt better

2) _____ had abdominal/reproductive issues reported healing and is now two months from giving birth

3) _____Asked for a baby, you prayed for LIFE in her womb. Later diagnosed with uterine cancer, and doctors wanted her to have hysterectomy. She did not have a hysterectomy, but had lots of prayer. Dr. just told her she does NOT have cancer. We are praying for a baby.

4) _____ played drums during prayer time when _____ and _____were healed. He noticed 2 days later that warts on his right hand had disappeared.

5) _____ back was healed of serious issues

6) _____ was healed of her bipolar disorder. Sounds like God really showed up. It is so neat to continue seeing God's healing touch.

Lucinda Teter

That is a good night of ministry, especially for the people who were healed. Items two, four, five and six all happened under the power and the anointing of our little healing "choo-choo" train.

Now let's fast-forward to October of the same year. My wife and I were ministering in Cornwall England at the Falmouth Light and Life Church led by Chris and Danutia Banwell. On Saturday evening, they coordinated a night of worship that served as a backdrop for a miracle service. This little church has an amazing spark of innocence, joy, creativity, and

wisdom like no little church I've ever seen. During the worship, Pastor Chris told me I had full freedom to do whatever the Lord told me to do. Those words were music to my ears because as the worship was well engaged, I was getting so filled with God's power; I was ready to gush forth from the very inner part of my being.

Now on the last and greatest day of the feast, Jesus stood and cried out, "If anyone is thirsty, let him come to me and drink! He who believes in me, as the Scripture has said, from within him will flow rivers of living water." But he said this about the Spirit, which those believing in him were to receive. John 7:37-39

After I preached, we went into a time of ministry and healing. The room was electric, and anticipation was high. Chris and Danutia have a gift for maintaining a free atmosphere perfect for healing and miracles. I called people forward in a line and then went down the line ministering one by one—one of the conveniences of small groups. About seventy or eighty people had attended this gathering, and about twenty of them were standing in the healing line. Worship was ablaze, and a few people were overflowing with joy and twitchy body language. I decided to try the same method that had worked so well in Kauai. I asked that handful of people I believed were manifesting God's power to come up. I would stand in front of the person seeking healing, ask what they needed, and then speak authoritatively against their sickness. As I did so, I would instruct the manifesting "ministry team" to squeeze the person's hands when the anointing felt strong. I would respond with a full-scale release of my entire spirit, imagining the living water flowing out of me onto the person being healed.

As we went down the line, I noticed a sophisticated-looking woman in her sixties standing behind the line observing as we ministered. She wasn't asking for ministry—in fact she looked reluctant to participate—but she was watching with interest. At one point, she closed her eyes and turned her palms up in a receiving stance. At that moment, our little electricity club was operating in full power and having the time of their life. As the power of God was flowing through the person who I was ministering to, the observing woman—who was standing about ten feet away—collapsed to the ground with a thud. It was as if she was a puppet and her strings had been cut. She lay out on the floor for a while and eventually got up and left the building. I discovered later that she was a local physician who had come to observe, hoping to be healed of an intestinal infirmity that was not succumbing to any other treatment. The next day she reported to our hosts that she left the room instantly healed.

A critic might say that these manifestations are partly due to the accepted and sometimes normal behavior of the charismatic Christian movement. But the following story lays that notion to rest.

In 2012 I was in the town of Anchorage Alaska. My friend Gary Wenzel and I were in the Anchorage

Mall walking around killing some time before we checked into the airport for our departure. Being an avid and lifelong surfer I made my way to the surf and skate shop. Gary decided to take a brisk walk around the mall for exercise. The mall was generally quite that morning and the surf shop was empty. The only two people in the store were the cashier and I. After a few minutes of perusing the store the cashier asked me if I was a local. This led into a conversation that ultimately led into a very dramatic God encounter. She began to tell me her story about moving to Alaska to take care of her ill mother. And she also opened up about her past failed relationships with men. The conversation went real deep, real fast. I asked her if anyone had ever shared the gospel of Jesus Christ with her. To my amazement the answer was no. In this day and age of all access information it is hard to imagine that anyone in America would not know the gospel. After asking a few questions I realized that she knew about Jesus and that He was the central figure of Christianity, but she did not know exactly why, nor did she understand the cross and the resurrection. So I asked her "would you like to know Him?" She said yes.

I warn you now that the rest of this story will offend you if you have a religious spirit and if you think that the only way to present the gospel is to explain it thoroughly and ask the girl to repeat the "sinners prayer". That is not what I did.

Instead I asked her to place her hand on the sales counter. At this moment I am obeying the impulses that I believe are being spoken into my mind from heaven. As soon as she placed her hand on the counter I placed my hand on her hand and looked her in the eye and said nothing. Within seconds her eyes began to fill with tears and her body tensed up. To my amazement she began to tremble and her tremble turn into shake. Her body shook intensely for at least one full minute. She shouted, "What is happening to me?" I responded, "this is God, and He is loving you". Then I received a word of knowledge about a certain sickness in her body. She affirmed that it was true so I told her that the Lord was healing that too. Her body continued to shake as we stood across the counter from one another with my hand on her hand. In the midst of that encounter some people had come into the store so I removed my hand and she rushed to the back office to regain her composure.

I left the store for a while and returned about 40 minutes later. There were still customers in the store but I could tell she wanted to speak to me so I waited. She asked again "what happened to me? I said, "you had an encounter with the God of the Bible and His Name is Jesus. Get to know him. And when you get home place the same hand that I laid my hand on, on your mother and the Lord will heal her too". She said, "Okay, I will". By then Gary had returned and we left for the airport.

This story eliminates the argument that the manifestation of being overwhelmed by presence of God to the point of uncontrollable shaking is intentional, fake or from another spirit. It also proves that we are capable of releasing the power of God by the laying on of hands. It is an honor and a joy to show the love of God with a demonstration of His power instead of trying to persuade her with information and beleifs. It is the difference between setting a seed on top of the soil where a bird or the wind can blow it away, verses setting the seed deep into the soil where it has a much better chance of growing and eventually blossoming. When a person is convinced into the kingdom they can be convinced out. Especially when they have no prior knowledge or foundation. But no person or spirit can take away a supernatural encounter with the manifest love of God.

My speech and my preaching were not in persuasive words of human wisdom, but in demonstration of the Spirit and of power, that your faith wouldn't stand in the wisdom of men, but in the power of God. 1st Corinthians 2:4-5

These testimonies are verifiable bearing the fruit of the Holy Spirit and the endorsement of heaven. In all of these a person could have been easily offended at the strange behavior. But each occurrence I described was orchestrated and obviously approved by God Himself; He healed and revealed Himself to people during this "strange behavior."

The Holy Spirit is God, and it is He who instructed me to do those things. I have no personal agenda, nor was I trying to prove a point. I was only presenting myself as a willing vessel available to the Lord for Him to accomplish His work in and through me. I merely did what I believed the Lord said, and I looked to the results for God's proof.

Therefore I urge you, brothers, by the mercies of God, to present your bodies a living sacrifice, holy, acceptable to God, which is your spiritual service. Don't be conformed to this world, but be transformed by the renewing of your mind, so that you may prove what is the good, well pleasing, and perfect will of God. Romans 12:1-2

Some would say that it is dangerous to approach Christianity with an "ends-justify-the-means" attitude. But this issue of so-called offensive and strange behavior is not an issue of sin or lust. Nor is it an issue of the nature of God, the cross, or salvation. This is a matter of opinion. It is detrimental to the kingdom of God and unfair to assume that a person overtaken by laughter or shaking is not or cannot be influenced by the Holy Spirit. I have discovered that whenever the Lord can manifest His power and love and at the same time make war against the demon spirit of religion, He will do so. God loves to kill two birds with one stone.

And the odd testimonies and manifestations I've mentioned are just the tip of the iceberg. The real scary stuff is actually in the Bible—don't forget Ezekiel. These people who manifest unusual behavior so easily are often indicators that God is present. They are the proverbial canaries in the gold mine.

Most of the laughers and the shakers and the twitchers and the bobbers are acutely aware of the dynamic presence of God. Their bodies are responding, and they have yielded themselves to this as an act of submission to the Lord. That's not to say the people who aren't doing this aren't manifesting God's presence in other ways. In fact, as someone who does not usually manifest visibly, I take very seriously the atmosphere of praise and worship and the behavior of those who do. Such behavior tells me that the wind of the Spirit is blowing. These people are like rustling of the leaves and the shaking of the limbs.

The wind blows where it wants to, and you hear its sound, but don't know where it comes from and where it is going. So is everyone who is born of the Spirit." Nicodemus answered him, "How can these things be?" Jesus answered him, "Are you the teacher of Israel, and don't understand these things? John 3:8-10

17. How The West Was Won

It would be impossible to muster up an entire history of this kind of Spirit-driven behavior that socially sophisticated cultures such as ours brand as unusual and some as heretic. And yet the entire Bible is filled with strange goings-on. A simple study of American history alone proves the normalcy of this, and it proves the benefit of it.

We don't have to go too far back to research the "Azusa Street Revival" or the "Toronto Blessing." These events are matters of history that are easily researched. Then there is the notorious life and times of the controversial personality, Lonnie Frisbee, who's raw and spontaneous methods of ministry sparked the entire Calvary Chapel movement and the Vineyard churches—both of which are now global organizations.

Lonnie was as unusual as they come. But the ripple effect of his ministry was, and still is, a massive gain for the glory of God and the Kingdom of heaven. To get a sense of Frisbee's heritage, I recommend the documentary film, *The Life And Death of A Hippie Preacher*.

I won't give a lengthy resource list here; you can easily research and prove the good that has come from such people and movements of God. I venture to say that most of you reading this book might very well discover that the impetus behind the movement or the church you call home originated with a display of signs, wonders, miracles and the very unusual behavior that go along with it.

What most Christians are unaware of is the dramatic impact these kinds of spiritual phenomena have had on the founding and success of not only Christianity as a whole but also on the formation and strengthening of the United States of America. In his national bestselling book, *A History of the American People*, Paul Johnson describes—without bias—the overall positive influence and impact early revival meetings had across America.

The first Great Awakening, largely fueled by the preaching of George Whitfield, began in the first half of the 1700s. Johnson says it "proved to be of vast significance, both in religion and in politics" and "it seems to have begun among the German immigrants, reflecting a spirit of thankfulness for their delivery from European poverty…."

Johnson also documents that Jonathan Edwards, preacher of the famous published sermon, Sinners In The Hands Of An Angry God, took over his father's church in Northampton Massachusetts. Johnson writes, "with no great success did he grow that congregation until he learned to base his message not so much on fear, as the old Puritan preachers did, as on joy." Johnson also adds: "It was part of Edwards' message that knowledge of God was education as well as revelation, that it was an aesthetic as well as a spiritual experience, and that it heightened the

senses." Edwards also preached with an eschatological bent towards "great events impending and that man-including American man- had a dramatic destiny."

The gatherings that formed around Edwards' preaching were filled with "fainting, weeping, and shrieking, which went on at the mass meetings and around the campfires."

Paul Johnson's observation is fundamental to my point in this chapter. In essence, Johnson observed that the first Great Awakening was fueled by the preaching of Jonathan Edwards and others who, as Johnson observes, taught that the knowledge of God leads to a revelation of God that literally heightens human senses. This observation comes from a facts-and-figures historian with no theological or political dog in the race. Johnson sums up the first Great Awakening by calling it a:

"Proto-revolutionary event, the formative moment in American history, preceding the political drive and making it possible. It crossed all religious and sectarian boundaries, made light of them indeed, and turned what had been a series of European-style churches into American ones."

To be proto-revolutionary is quite a concept. In essence Johnson is saying that the first Great Awakening was the *spiritual* beginning of the American Revolution. The external manifestation of unusual spiritual behavior resulted in the Americanizing of European-style Christianity.

Johnson quotes this incredible statement by John Adams:

"The Revolution was affected before the war commenced. The Revolution was in the mind and the hearts of the people: and change in their religious sentiments of their duties and obligations."

Johnson goes on to say that the American Revolution itself was:

"A marriage between the rationalism of the American elites touched by the Enlightenment with the spirit of the Great Awakening among the masses which enabled the popular enthusiasm thus aroused to be channeled into the political aims of the Revolution-itself soon identified as the coming eschatological event. Neither force could have succeeded without the other. The Revolution could not have taken place without this religious background."

The second wave of the Great Awakening produced even more and stranger behavior, including testimonies of music literally coming out of human bodies, without the person singing. Let me rephrase for clarity: the music did not come from their mouths, but from their bodies. Johnson says "such music silenced everything."

Now let me condense the previous two pages for you. Preachers like Whitfield, Edwards, and others stir up passion in the hearts of men and women to the point that they abandon established religious norms and open up to the move of the Holy Spirit. Remember,

those meetings were filled with "fainting, weeping and shrieking" and—best of all—*musical bodies.* I think it's safe to say that such things qualify as "strange behavior" and the "supernatural." [15]

That movement of God spread across the country like a fire and literally unified the American people to the point that President John Adams saw it as a catalyst for our success in the American Revolution. Wow! The next time I see someone shaking and falling down under the power of the Holy Spirit, I'm going to say to myself: *here comes the revolution.*

By their fruits you will know them. Do you gather grapes from thorns, or figs from thistles? Even so, every good tree produces good fruit; but the corrupt tree produces evil fruit. A good tree can't produce evil fruit, neither can a corrupt tree produce good fruit. Every tree that doesn't grow good fruit is cut down, and thrown into the fire. Therefore by their fruits you will know them. Matthew 7:16-20

With all this in mind, a case could be made that the "taking of mountains" that Dr. Lance Wallnau[16] talks about starts with national revival and Holy Spirit outpour. This shared experience becomes a catalyst that provides the perfect blend of boldness tempered in humility.

---

[15] History of the American People by Paul Johnson pg.112-117, 296

[16] Lancewallnau.com

As odd as it may sound, the strange manifestations and behavior of Revival actually becomes the depository of kingdom breakthrough, influence and resources. Powerful moves of God create Mega-shifts personally, corporately and nationally. It is best that we embrace them. Revival is the beginning of things to come, not the end in-and-of itself.

18. Appetite For Worship

One of the key elements to living a supernatural Christian lifestyle is the act of worship. Since miracles happen in the presence of God, the presence of God is where we must exist on a continual basis. Not for the sake of the miracles alone but also for the sheer pleasure of worshiping the One who is worthy of our praise. It is in the context of this exchange that the presence of God is amplified and can even manifest as the Lord responds to our praise.

But you are holy, you who inhabit the praises of Israel. Psalm 22:3

This dynamic worship atmosphere is where we can learn to recognize presence as our spirit is literally flowing with the properties of heaven and the Spirit of God. In such an atmosphere, we develop an acute sensitivity to God's presence, which is invaluable to our overall spiritual life. God is omnipresent, and we can encounter Him anywhere, but He is also able and desirous of amplifying Himself for those who hunger for more of Him. The entire Bible is basically a history book filled with stories of ordinary men and women who were graced with a non-typical hunger for the presence of God. And it is this hunger for God that drives us to the apex of our Christian experience. Worship.

Corporate worship is truly the great exchange between heaven and earth. You may or may not be aware of this, but when we worship God, we are actually united with the citizenry of heaven. As we worship God, our supernatural lifestyle takes on a reciprocal nature in real time because there is a special non-duplicable dynamic in the corporate gathering of praise and worship that you cannot get anywhere else, nor can God Himself get it any other way. Corporate praise is a gift to heaven from earth that unites the two into one. Worship is when that which is on earth becomes, as it is in heaven in a grand scale.

My approach to worship is this: it is the place where I bring my confession and contrition to God's throne, receive my grace and forgiveness, become overwhelmed by His goodness, give Him the glory and honor that He deserves, and walk away justified. I don't want to come off as legalistic, but worship is where I personally go to deliver to my God that which I owe Him. I try to refrain from *praying* too long when I worship, but rather stay focused on *praising* and *honoring*. Sometimes I just can't help it, and I bring my requests to the Lord during a time of worship, but when I do, I try to make it brief. Although prayer is almost always infused into my worship, I consciously try to steer my heart back into praise. It doesn't take long to say what I need to say in regards to prayer requests or sin confession, but who can count the number of ways we can praise Him?

I rarely accomplish this, but I aim to spend 90% of my worship time simply praising Him with no questions asked and no requests made.

It would be safe for me to conclude that the Old Testament and the New Testament each have their most popular personalities. David the Son of Jesse is without doubt the shining star and spiritual prodigy of the Old Testament, and the apostle Paul is the undisputed champion of the New Testament. I find it interesting that each of them have their "one thing" statement—the crowning emphasis that branded them and motivated them towards their destinies. David wrote:

One thing I have asked of Yahweh, that I will seek after: that I may dwell in Yahweh's house all the days of my life, to see Yahweh's beauty, and to inquire in his temple. Psalm 27:4

That is incredible! David is petitioning God to grant him the option to spend his entire existence in the direct presence of God beholding His beauty. Imagine what it would be like to be so passionate about worship and so desirous to spend every waking hour beholding the beauty of the Lord that we ask the Lord to orchestrate our lives in such a way that we never have to leave the altar of praise.

I wonder: can we accomplish the great commission by worshipping God and doing nothing else? It is possible, but we would have to expand our understanding of worship and all it entails. For instance, work itself is an act of worship. Giving is an act of worship, and so on. You get the point.

On the other hand, the apostle Paul had an entirely different emphasis. Or did he?

Brothers, I don't regard myself as yet having taken hold, but one thing I do. Forgetting the things which are behind, and stretching forward to the things which are before, I press on toward the goal for the prize of the high calling of God in Christ Jesus. Philippians 3:13-14

An examination of scripture reveals that Paul was a man on an Apostolic, gospel-spreading mission. The entire thrust of Paul's post-Jesus-encounter life was to preach the gospel to the entire Roman Empire while also reaching as many Jews as he could along the way.

Paul was eventually imprisoned because of his relentless pursuit of this cause. If Paul had not appealed to Caesar while in prison he could have been freed:

Agrippa said to Festus, "This man might have been set free if he had not appealed to Caesar." Acts 26:32

But Paul was determined to take the gospel to Caesar, knowing that it may cost him his life. And it did.

Here is my point. A careful examination of the life of David and Paul will prove that both were diligent champions who relentlessly pursued and achieved

God's call upon their lives. The Lord singled them each out, and each responded in obedience. Yet their unique personalities and different senses of priority expose a tension. Paul was narrowly focused on his mission with what could be labeled as a martyr's complex. And the Lord used him. Paul was so bent on the salvation of the entire nation of Israel that he was willing to forfeit his own. He said:

I tell the truth in Christ. I am not lying, my conscience testifying with me in the Holy Spirit, ² that I have great sorrow and unceasing pain in my heart. ³ For I could wish that I myself were accursed from Christ for my brothers' sake, my relatives according to the flesh, ⁴ who are Israelites; Romans 9:1-3

David, the gifted King and man of war preferred to spend his entire life *beholding God's beauty and enquiring in His temple.* Both men were champions. Both achieved the will of God. Each had a completely different approach to God.

Recognizing these kinds of tension in Scripture, and finding the gem that often dangles in between them, often results in the discovery of a deep, biblical revelation. And I believe I found the relevant gem to my premise in a statement Jesus Himself made:

As they went on their way, he entered into a certain village, and a certain woman named Martha received him into her house. She had a sister called Mary, who also sat at Jesus' feet, and heard his word. But Martha was distracted with much serving, and she came up to

143

him, and said, "Lord, don't you care that my sister left me to serve alone? Ask her therefore to help me." Jesus answered her, "Martha, Martha, you are anxious and troubled about many things, but one thing is needed. Mary has chosen the good part, which will not be taken away from her." Luke 10:38-41

Jesus' "one thing" is that worship takes priority over all. For the record, no person in human history can match the determination Jesus modeled as His whole life was spent intentionally en route to the cross, pursuing the will of the Father with great precision. Therefore, Paul lived a very Christ-like life and died a Christ-like death. But Jesus said what He said about Mary because He meant it. And I agree. Worship is the "one thing" needed, or as David put it: "to behold the beauty of the Lord."

Is it possible that the apostle Paul was not prototypical of the normal Christian life? When Jesus appeared to Ananias in a vision and commissioned him to help the newly converted Paul, Jesus described Paul as:

"my chosen vessel to bear my name before the nations and kings, and the children of Israel. ¹⁶ For I will show him how many things he must suffer for my name's sake." Acts 9:15-16

The message of the Gospel was a God-infused obsession with Paul, and his primary mission was to spread it relentlessly at the cost of everything—including his health. Paul's sole goal was spreading

the Gospel of a resurrected Jesus, especially among religious and political leaders. This was a task that Jesus Himself avoided.

We do not all carry the same kingdom assignment in regards to the role we play in the spreading of the gospel; therefore worship is the actual "one thing" that we all share as a mandate. It is our ministry to the Lord. And we, like David, must pursue the heart of God. It is from worship experiences and encounters where most of us will draw our strength, sustenance, joy, peace, and our power. Jesus said, "If any man thirst, let him come unto me and drink." And there is no better way to approach our Lord for the infilling of life-giving water than to come to Him in praise.

A lifestyle of worship empowers the supernatural Christian life. When we worship as a company of saints, we plug into a corporate anointing and blessing that I believe compounds our take-away from the experience. And that take-away is usually only realized in the aftermath. Corporate worship increases our anointing, thus our ability to accomplish the will of God for our individual lives. Worship must be a consistent and central theme of our life so that we, like David, live in a constant desire to "behold the beauty of the Lord" and, like Mary, prefer sitting at Jesus feet over "serving" the Lord. In that place of yielded submission, the big battles are won: the battles that wage inside us over our own sin, pride, lust, attitudes, etc. Not to mention the battles for our families, ministries, and finances. Beholding the beauty of the Lord and sitting at His feet in praise and adoration is where most crucial battles are won. Worship must become a lifestyle.

19. Developing Your Worship Life

Since worship is a vital discipline of the Christian life, have you ever considered the idea of improving and developing your worship life? In the same way you would improve and develop other skills and disciplines you can qualitatively improve your worship. In the world of culinary arts the way food is displayed on a plate is called the Presentation. Consider your worship as a kind of internal presentation before the Lord.

Whenever we enter into the sanctuary of praise, we come with a precondition: an attitude. If there is something upsetting us internally—such as a conflict with another person or a business situation—that tension is the precondition we enter into praise with. And it affects our "presentation". We can all fill in the blank with a plethora of potential obstacles that could obstruct the flow from our heart to God's heart. Our precondition is the starting point for our worship. Our job is to get to the place where the distractions we brought into the worship experience are placed into their proper context, and the negative influences on our heart and mind eliminated. This is particularly difficult when we are facing dire circumstances or, on the flip side, when our lives are so blessed that the blessing itself has a dulling effect on our passion. David was referred to as a "man after

God's own heart".[17] I used to think this meant that God sought for a man who had a heart like His. But in its original Hebrew, the phrase "sought him a man after his own heart" was only three words: *Baqash Iysh Lebab.*[18] It translates to: "The Lord seeks for a heart that seeks His heart." Saul did not seek the heart of God but rather let circumstances dictate his actions, as in 1 Samuel 13. But David, who definitely had some notable lapses of character, pursued the heart of God with passion. Worship can be exactly that: an intentional pursuit of the heart of God. On this pursuit, I have to fill my mind with truth. I often find myself spending the first few minutes of worship casting down lies and replacing those thoughts with what God really thinks about me and what He has said to me. Not what some lying, deceiving voice in my head is saying; but what God has already said. In some cases this battle may take up the entire worship session.

For though we walk in the flesh, we don't wage war according to the flesh; for the weapons of our warfare are not of the flesh, but mighty before God to the throwing down of strongholds, throwing down imaginations and every high thing that is exalted against the knowledge of God, and bringing every thought into captivity to the obedience of Christ; 2 Corinthians 10:3-5

---

[17] 1 Samuel 13:11-14

[18] Strongs Concordance

If the gateway to my mind is under attack when I begin to worship, I will often meditate on this verse and others until these truths become my truth. I am after God's heart! Not philosophically or symbolically. I mean this in a very real and literal sense. I will fight and wage war in the arena of my own heart and mind until my heart connects with His heart. My desire is to see what God sees, hear what God hears, and seek God's will for that exact moment. I don't want to miss whatever it is He wants to do and say right when He wants to do it and say it. That is my desire for the entire worship experience. But first, I have to slay anything vain or detrimental. All self-flagellation and condemnation must go. I clear out and then press in.

20. The Art Of Pressing In

Every Sunday morning all around the world, churches are filled with worshippers. The style and form of worship varies from the singing of timeless, classic hymns to the modern, simpler choruses introduced by the Jesus People movement of the early 1970s. Today, there is a worship movement based in Sacramento, California called Jesus Culture. They fill arenas around the world with mostly young people singing praise to God. Jesus Culture songs are lyrically simple and sparse but rich in depth and passion. The songs draw people into a God consciousness that is engaging and refreshing. Worshippers of all denominations and backgrounds enjoy Jesus Culture.

Jesus Culture Music creates the kind of worship I've been talking about. They have fine-tuned the worship experience into what I call "the art of pressing in." This is nothing new, nor is it a worship fad. From the moment the earth was created until this very day, humanity's desire and passion to draw near to God in the form of song and dance has been alive and well. Every epoch in history has found its way to the throne of God's presence because in the very heart of each person is the desire to experience God. It is this very real need in our emotional and spiritual being that has driven each of us to seek Him. This "one thing" connects us all. We have been graced with a hunger for more of God that motivates us to rearrange our lives to be in proximity to His throne of grace. And we must press in. But what does this look like? How do we press in? How can we do so, no matter what church we worship in, no matter what style of praise we sing, and no matter how we feel at the moment of engagement?

For you to reach your destiny in Christ, you must break free of the social and societal pressures around you that keep you boxed in and bound. For some of you, that pressure is more of a personal restraint, and for others the pressure of conformity has been imposed upon you. No matter the situation, you must discover a way to push past whatever limitation besets you and narrow your focus in pursuit of His throne until you achieve breakthrough. It's not about lifting hands or kneeling or bowing, it's about your willingness to yield to the Spirit impulses that ultimately position you to become a victorious worshipper. To become that worshipper, you must obey the voice of the Lord and the leading of the Holy Spirit, trust your sanctified imagination, and lavish your praise and your love upon your God—the One who first pursued you with an offering of sacrifice. The One who first celebrated you and danced and spun in the joy of knowing you. Yes, God danced in anticipation of this moment with you.

Remember the Proverbs 8 view into the pre-incarnate world of Jesus? It revealed him dancing and spinning in the splendor and glory of God the Father celebrating us: His most beloved possession. Jesus said, "My delight was with the sons of men"! And it

is. One of Jesus' names is Emanuel, meaning 'God with us'.

This is why we worship. *This* is whom we praise. Jesus danced and spun in anticipation of being with us. Like begets like: kisses invite kisses, hugs invite hugs, dance invites dance, and love invites more love. Our worship offering unto the Lord must ultimately draw us into a dance with Him. *This* is true worship.

For where two or three are gathered together in my name, there I am in the middle of them. Matthew 18:20

Am I saying we must literally break out in dance? Maybe. I *am* saying that we are headed to what Martin Smith so perfectly described as "Gods Great Dance Floor." Whether you are at home in the secret place, on the mountaintop, in the city park, or on the upholstered church chair, you must respond. God will join you, and heaven will open. New avenues of prayer will open up and new realms of thought released. The spiritual forces that have been assigned to destroy you will be scattered. The angelic beings assigned to protect you will be released en masse—chasing the demons off into the desert places where they can howl at the moon in defeat. Because once again the Lords beloved has stepped out onto the floor of praise, joy, and honor, and the Prince who delights to be with you will once again mark you as untouchable.

This is your offense, defense, and game plan. Worship is your joy and your mission. It is your primary ministry unto the Lord and your present and future existence in Him. Become relentless as you practice the art of pressing in. It is the portal into your future.

21. Pray It Forward

There comes a time for each of us when our routine prayer and worship is not enough to motivate heaven to respond. I assume all believers have a prayer life. Sometimes it sounds like this: "I meet with God while I am driving to work," or "I meet with God in the morning while I have my coffee," or "I meet with God just before I go to bed." These are daily rituals we might label prayer or devotions. They are all good, and we should keep doing them. But!

What do we do differently when we r-e-a-l-l-y need to meet with God? How does our prayer and worship life change when life's circumstances drive us desperately to God, beseeching Him to act on our behalf? What do we do when the demand upon our life or ministry requires dramatic and precise intervention from the throne of heaven? Or what about those times when you just need a close encounter from the Lord, a healing touch from His loving hand, or an increased measure of anointing for the road that lay ahead? In such moments, we must develop a strategy that differs in tone, atmosphere, timing—and even location—from our normal routine of prayer and worship.

It is essential that we learn to press in to the throne of God in our prayer life too. There are those times when we cannot wait on Him to show up, but instead we must go to Him. And I say with confidence: the

Lord has life-changing encounters waiting in reserve for us that will only be realized in our relentless pursuit of Him. These encounters will not be handed to us on a silver platter. I'd like to suggest that dynamic prayer and praise gets dynamic results. To be clear, it's not about volume or motion but more about purpose and drive: if you desire to live a supernatural lifestyle, then you must develop an offensive approach to spirituality and prayer. There are times to pray in a stance of rest and there are times to pray in pursuit. And if you watch any sports team, you know that the offense is much more fun than defense. Especially when the defensive strategy of the opposition has become weakened and exposed.

We must become fervent and passionate about personal breakthrough, increased anointing, spiritual gifts, and callings. Stop drifting through life wondering when the next encounter will come your way. Like Jesus, your "meat is to do the will of him that sent me, and to finish his work" [19]

You become the initiating—and at times aggressive— warrior, stirring up the spiritual realm around you. Stop sitting back just reading your Bible every day waiting for Jesus to come back, and start expanding His kingdom by destroying the works of the devil, thus establishing a lifestyle that is less prone to spiritual attack, sickness, and disease. This kind of

---

[19] John 4:34.

lifestyle actually draws on the resources of heaven to accomplish the will of the Father. Using the sports analogy, it is possible to *regain control of the ball*. This means switching to offensive spirituality instead of the exhaustion of constant defense. And this is done through aggressive forward thinking prayer and worship that literally presses into the realm of the spirit, causing heaven to respond in an area that might otherwise remain unaffected. I'm talking about praying forward with passion:

...when he had offered one sacrifice for sins forever, sat down on the right hand of God; from that time waiting until his enemies are made the footstool of his feet. For by one offering he has perfected forever those who are being sanctified". Hebrews 10:12-14

This is incredible! Jesus currently sits at the right hand of God the Father *waiting until his enemies are made his footstool.* And it appears that the following phrase is an allusion to who is responsible for carrying out that job: *those who are being sanctified."*

If we really believe prayer changes things, then why not pray the future? My son and I opened a new business recently. We've only been open a few months, but we have started the first Monday of each month with a simple, to-the-point prayer for the month. This prayer time is less focused on whatever we may be dealing with that day and more concentrated on how we would like the oncoming month to play-out. We are determined to maintain control of the ball. And offensive, anticipatory prayer is one of our strategies. The same goes for personal and ministry-related prayer. I prefer to thank the Lord for yesterday's blessings, forget the defeats, and talk about tomorrow.

22. Grace Revisited

Let's therefore draw near with boldness to the throne of grace, that we may receive mercy, and may find grace for help in time of need. Hebrews 4:16

Grace for the believer is empowerment to do His will, like an endorsement from heaven. When we came to Christ in repentance, God's grace was applied to all of our past, present, and future sins. Then, once we are *in* the Kingdom, that same grace becomes our power. Therefore, we press in boldly for the grace to do His will. And it is in that pressing mode that something happens: an exchange between heaven and earth during which grace becomes realized—sometimes in a very dramatic fashion. Once a person is saved or "born again"[20] grace and anointing are two sides of the same coin so-to-speak. And when grace comes the atmosphere shifts, and the presence of the Lord manifests. Our bodies may become weak or faint, sometimes quivering as the power of God is released into us. We may become overwhelmed with the fear of God like Isaiah[21] and say, "I am a man of unclean lips." Or we may respond in praise and worship as we realize that He has responded to our desire and has come down on our behalf. Such a moment is different than our typical morning coffee prayer time, different than our brief moments in the

[20] John 3:3

[21] Isaiah 6:5

car on our way to work. Either we have been caught up into heaven or heaven has come down to us. Either way is good. When this kind of encounter happens, we discover the power of pressing in verses waiting for Him to meet us along the way.

I am on the prayer ministry team at my church. Every Sunday I stand up front with a line of 40 to 50 prayer servants, ministering to individuals who come forward for prayer. The number one request is a desire for more of God. They make that request plain and simple without hesitation. Many have traveled halfway around the world to be prayed for. And more often than not, they get what they came for. Is it because they had a destiny with me? Of course not! The exchange between them and I is a point of contact that the Holy Spirit is more than happy to honor. It is the hunger and the passion within that person that caused them to travel to our city, come forward for prayer, and make the request for "more" of God. This encounter that often takes place as a result of their request is an act of grace. It is a gift from heaven that was paid for on the cross by Jesus Christ. And now, with great passion and sincerity, this person is coming to Jesus for a greater measure of His grace. They want to experience God and be filled with the Holy Spirit so they can accomplish the will of God in their own life. And the Lord grants them the desire of their hearts. Grace comes upon them in great power, often causes their limbs to grow weak and a sensation of low voltage (and sometimes not-so-low voltage) electricity to run through their body. The Spirit of the living God increases inside of

them, and every emotion they have is activated as they surrender to this moment of empowering grace.

It is a shame that much of the Church is offended and critical of the phenomena called "slain in the spirit." I was one of those critics for many years. And I am ashamed of my judgment. Now, when I see this happen or when I lay hands on a person in prayer and they fall to the ground, I think to myself: *grace has come.* And grace equals the power to do His will. It is that simple.

Who are you, great mountain? Before Zerubbabel you are a plain; and he will bring out the capstone with shouts of 'Grace, grace, to it!' Zechariah 4:7

23. God Is One And We Can Know Them

"When the Comforter has come, whom I will send to you from the Father, the Spirit of truth, who proceeds from the Father, he will testify about me. John 15:26

The word "testify" is a translation from the Greek word *martyreo*. It means, "to bear witness, affirm, teach by revelation and conjure." That last word especially interested me; to conjure is "to make appear." An encounter with the person of the Holy Spirit can and often does lead into a encounter with the person of Jesus Christ.

When we engage the Holy Spirit with a conscious and verbal recognition of His personhood, not ignoring His identity as being separate from the Father and the Son, there is a strong possibility that the person of Jesus Christ becomes dramatically amplified and can even manifest to varying degrees. This was the very path I was on during the Jesus encounter I wrote about in chapter 11. I am convinced that had I not corrected my relationship with the person of the Holy Spirit, that particular encounter with Jesus would not have happened. If I were to say, "God, I just want to know you more." God could justifiably answer "*Who* more?" Our Christian language and habitual vernacular have diluted the power of the separate identities of the three persons of God.

Why is this important? The supernatural lifestyle requires interaction and personal history with all three persons of God. Each of the three persons of God has tendencies and personality traits and attributes that you want to know and recognize. And each of them plays different roles in the miraculous. I'm not saying that we can't or shouldn't address God in a general sense, too, but I *am* saying that we can serve the world, the Church, and the Kingdom of Heaven much better by learning to direct our prayers and conversations precisely to the one we are speaking with.

This simple adjustment also helps you to discern those moments when the presence of God is near and upon you. Who is it that has drawn near to you? The Father, the Son or the Holy Spirit? Knowing whom we are addressing will help shape our conversation, thus causing us to pray and dialogue with God in a more precise manner.

And precision counts. Please don't misunderstand what I am saying here. God is not rigid; He understands exactly who we are and how we are aware of Him…and He is more than happy to work in that context. But, the more we get to know each of the three persons of God, the Father, Son and Holy Ghost as individuals, the more approachable and diverse this One God becomes. And it can and will shape the way we spend our time with Him and the way we pray.

At a very young age, children have the ability to discern the presence of God and respond accordingly. From conversations with my own grandchildren, I have come to realize that children understand the difference between a Holy Spirit manifestation, a Jesus encounter, and time spent with the Father. This is because they aren't old enough for misguided doctrine and limitations about God to infect their minds. I highly recommend Jennifer Toledo's book, *Children And The Supernatural*.

A wealth of potential breakthrough awaits us in the spiritual realm when we learn to fine-tune our interpersonal relationship with each person of God. We don't have one relationship with God; we have *three* relationships. And they are all worthy of our time, our effort, our study, and our praise. This discovery may uncover some hurtful but needful truths. I myself had no idea that I really didn't know the Holy Spirit until I read Benny Hinn's book *Welcome, Holy Spirit*. When I read it, I had been a pastor for sixteen years. I could have taught you all about the Holy Spirit and His gifts. But I didn't know Him. I also came to realize I barely knew the Father. I came out of the Jesus People movement, so Jesus was my *everything* so-to-speak. Literally. I thought I knew the other two persons of God, but I only knew about them as they relate to Jesus. God was gracious during that time and now I realize that the Father and the Holy Spirit were anxious and desirous to be known by me too.

Entire Christian movements have even labeled themselves according to which person of God they best relate. The Calvary Chapel movement, birthed in Southern California in the early 1970s, is often referred to as the "Jesus People" movement. The Toronto Airport Revival, known for it's outpouring of joy and laughter, has developed and shared a powerful and keen understanding of the "Father heart of God." Pastor John Arnott, who helped usher in that movement, wrote a book about the Toronto Blessing called *The Father's Blessing.*

It makes sense that, at certain times in history, God would emphasize one person of Himself over another to make large-scale adjustments in the Church as a whole. Because of such evidence, I conclude that one element of Christian maturity is the ability to know each person of God, to relate to each of them, and to speak to each of them as individuals while simultaneously comprehending them as one God.

We usually enter into the Kingdom with a semi-understanding of one of the three persons of God. This is typically Jesus, since "in Him dwells all the fullness of God bodily".[22] And from that foundation, we discover God in His entirety.

The following story is an example of one very dramatic encounter I had with the person of the Holy Spirit that helped open me up to this understanding

---

[22] Colossians 2:9

and helped shape the way I interacted with God. One Saturday, as I was preparing my Sunday sermon, I had so many emotions, needs, and things I wanted to communicate to God that it was impossible for me to say what I needed to say. Even speaking in tongues felt limiting. I was in our church alone. I realized that the Holy Spirit was present, and I sensed an overcoming presence. I felt overshadowed. It wasn't Jesus in the room nor was it God the Father. It was like the Holy Spirit was in me and on me, leading me into what became a very bizarre form of prayer. I began to make up my own sign language with my hands, and that developed into a dance as I groaned and allowed sounds to rise from the innermost part of my being to emerge from my mouth. This unusual combination of body motion and sounds went on for about an hour. Up until that time, I had been so perplexed and confined by things in my life and in the church that I was at a spiritual, emotional, and intellectual standstill. And now this unusual form of prayer and intercession became my release.

As the encounter continued, I moved out of the prayer room into the sanctuary. The building was empty, and I could do whatever I wanted, so I just let go and yielded to the Holy Spirit. At times I would drop to the ground and bow in worship, then I would suddenly get up as if totally under the influence of sheer impulse. I began to dance and twist and bend, moving my hands with symbolic gestures again. I knew that I was interacting with the person of the Holy Spirit. He and I were one. I knew that what was happening was a legitimate form of prayer. I could tell that things were being drawn out of me like a supernatural vacuum clearing my heart and mind. The limitation of words and speech had been removed, and I was connecting directly to heaven. All of the heavy stuff inside of me was being drawn out as the peace of God was being put in. It was tangible, it was real, and it set me free to move forward with my day.

That particular kind of encounter has only happened a few times in my life, and each time was quite exhausting and effective. The Holy Spirit was actually guiding me into these movements and sounds, thus pulling prayer out of me.

In the same way, the Spirit also helps our weaknesses, for we don't know how to pray as we ought. But the Spirit himself makes intercession for us with groanings, which can't be uttered. He who searches the hearts knows what is on the Spirit's mind, because he makes intercession for the saints according to God. Romans 8:26

Some Bible translations [23] say "according to the will of God" which is not accurate. It removes God from the equation and inserts His will instead.

Remember that the Holy Spirit comes directly *from* the Father. This means that when I acted out my very dramatic prayer-dance, the Spirit who was making

---

[23] KJV, NKJV, NASB

intercession for me according to God who had searched my heart was leading me. In other words, the Father took note of my frustration and sent the Holy Spirit. The Holy Spirit was leading according to God. Not according to the *will* of God but according to *God*. It is like God gave the Holy Spirit the sheet music, the Holy Spirit was the conductor, and I was the entire orchestra. And the resulting music was a dramatic symphony that started off sad and bewildered and ended with a grand crescendo of victory, triumph, and praise.

God, in His infinite wisdom, has chosen to manifest Himself in multiple persons, thus making Himself more accessible and available at every level of consciousness and awareness. This opens up entire realms of thought, prayer, and praise. God is One God, and our quest is to know *Them*.

24. You Are The Greatest

If we desire to be a voice for change and transformation in people and culture we must have a strong sense of identity. And a good start is to realize that you are the greatest! Now let me explain. Speaking of John the Baptist, The apostle John described John the Baptist like this:

There came a man, sent from God, whose name was John. The same came as a witness that he might testify about the light, that all might believe through him. John 1:6-7

Later on, Jesus Himself described John the Baptist, saying: *"For I tell you, among those who are born of women there is not a greater prophet than John the Baptizer, yet he who is least in God's Kingdom is greater than he." Luke 7:28*

According to Jesus, the moment we are spiritually born into the kingdom of God, we are greater than the greatest prophet ever "born of women." I ask you to accept that statement at face value without explaining all the reasons why it is true. It's true because Jesus said it. My entire point of this chapter is to establish that you have great prophet potential.

Realizing the prophetic anointing that rests on you is essential for developing and operating in that gift. Not every believer holds the office of a prophet, but every person in the kingdom is a greater prophet than John the Baptist. The gift of prophecy is a powerful tool and a weapon. You need to tap into your prophetic gift so you can be an agent of change for a better future.

The question is: what does prophecy look like for the average Christian? Is it big grandiose statements about the end of the world or the errors and pending judgment of the Church? No, it is not! Your prophetic ministry is for the purpose of encouraging those around you and allowing God to use you to speak for Him to the world around you. This is part of the supernatural lifestyle: it's receiving and giving His goodness. And His goodness *is* the message. And if you are harsh to others or speak damning words of doom to them, the Holy Spirit will stop speaking to you and you will be on your own. The gospel is *good* news.

But he who prophesies speaks to men for their edification, exhortation, and consolation.
1 Corinthians 14:3

The following verse taken from the Book of Joel is understood by me to be a prophecy referring to the final return of Jesus Christ. If this is the case, and I believe it is, then Jesus Himself will be offering amnesty and grace to those who have rebelled against Him at His return. This is one of my positions about the return of Jesus. I believe he will offer forgiveness to those who don't know Him and are alive when He

comes back. I'm not saying there isn't a hell. I am saying Jesus is full of grace, even at His return.

Yahweh thunders his voice before his army; for his forces are very great; for he is strong who obeys his command; for the day of Yahweh is great and very awesome, and who can endure it? Yet even now," says Yahweh, "turn to me with all your heart, and with fasting, and with weeping, and with mourning." Tear your heart, and not your garments, and turn to Yahweh, your God; for he is gracious and merciful, slow to anger, and abundant in loving kindness, and relents from sending calamity. Who knows? He may turn and relent, and leave a blessing behind him,

Joel 2:11-14

If Jesus Himself is willing to *"turn and relent, and leave a blessing"* right smack in the middle of His triumphant return when He is in final judgment mode then we know that genuine repentance can shape and even re-shape the present and the future. Judgment belongs to the Lord not you or me, therefore we should learn to speak and prophesy towards the desired positive outcome rather than echoing the trend of assumed pending doom. And for the record this is not positive confession, but rather prophetic declaration. And there is a vast difference. When our prophetic declarations are in tune with the heart of God they are powerful and authoritative.

I do understand that there are Gods unchangeable prophecies concerning future events. Unfortunately many prophecy experts so-called have the habit of reading into Bible prophecies things that just aren't there. We cannot forget that God wants His people (us) to be influencers and participants in the future. We have the authority and even the mandate to turn the tide of future events in more spheres of influence and realms of society and government than we currently do. A realization and activation of this single truth alone can save an entire nation. Possibly yours ☺

I venture to say that one of the riskiest things a supernatural culture does is empower and encourage people to prophesy. But it is a necessary risk. The Lord is anxious to get you moving in your prophetic gift because He has so much blessing and encouragement to say to His church and to the world. Once your prophetic gift is activated, you will find yourself speaking into situations you never imagined yourself involved in.

After church one Sunday, friends asked me to give a prophetic word to some of their friends who were visiting from South Africa. I responded, "sure" with a smile on my face, all the while cringing on the inside. I had no knowledge whatsoever of these people, and within sixty seconds after meeting them, I had already forgotten their names. Though I knew it was an honor to be asked in such a direct manner to prophesy, I always get a little nervous in that kind of situation. I know its because I want to get it right and I take even the most random moments seriously. Typically my prophetic style is precise and to the

point. For example, I once told a man that I saw a lemon tree hovering over him. I did not know that an hour prior to me meeting him for the first time, he and his wife were at Home Depot shopping for lemon trees. He asked what my vision meant. I said, "Buy the tree and find out." I have dozens and dozens of similar stories.

But I still get nervous. The couple from South Africa was very receptive and easy to talk to. I placed my hand on the husband's shoulder and closed my eyes as we all stood there in silence waiting for God to speak...through me. In my mind's eye, I saw a map of the United States on a wall with colored pins stuck on it. And the words came to mind, "The Lord says yes." So I described what I was seeing. Their response wasn't enthusiastic, although I could tell they were pleased in a quiet way. I assumed the vision was a confirmation for them to take some kind of road trip. This is why I rarely interpret these kinds of open visions. I would have been very wrong in my interpretation.

The next day was the first day of a conference at our church. I was standing in the back; just hanging around, when this same gentleman approached me. He was in a good mood and had been searching for me. He explained to me that he was an oil executive representing a firm based in South Africa. He said that in his office hung a map of the United States with markers along a certain highways in the Midwest. Each marker represented a potential drilling site for oil. And according to my prophetic word, the Lord had said "yes." My first thought was: *should I give him my mailing address so he knows where to send the check?*

It would be impossible to overstate the power of the gift of words of knowledge and prophecy. Both demonstrate the power of God and are near-tangible proof that a voice outside of the realm of time, space, and matter is communicating to us.

When you are on the receiving end this kind of intentional and personal prophecy you never know where things can lead from there. I call it the moment of *prophetic reception.* Meaning the moment you hear, receive and agree with the prophecy spoken over you.

One Tuesday during a meeting at my church, my pastor came up behind me and symbolically placed a cloak on my shoulders. He then said, "The Lord is giving you a Joseph anointing." Not long after that—due to an unusual turn of events that I can't elaborate on—I was invited into a home of a very wealthy family for a weekend to minister healing, give impartation, and to prophesy. At about 11 pm on the first evening, I was awakened from sleep and asked to be part of a Skype conference and offer words of knowledge and prophecy on a business deal. It was a pending three-trillion-dollar gold transaction between two countries. I can't say any more, but the reason I share this is to reveal how desirous the world is for those who will yield their prophetic gift to the

Lord and determine themselves to be ambassadors of His goodness.

A person, business or institution can even be fast-tracked into a greater realm of the supernatural and will experience greater miracles from the moment of prophetic reception. There are added benefits that come when we receive a word as from the Lord into our heart and respond accordingly.

The following Bible text is about the first time Jesus met Nathanael. You will observe that Jesus gave him a word of knowledge that not only transformed him into an instant believer in Jesus Christ and His kingdom, but also set Nathanael on a course towards "greater things" and an *open heaven* encounter.

On the next day, he was determined to go out into Galilee, and he found Philip. Jesus said to him, "Follow me." Now Philip was from Bethsaida, of the city of Andrew and Peter. Philip found Nathanael, and said to him, "We have found him, of whom Moses in the law, and the prophets, wrote: Jesus of Nazareth, the son of Joseph." Nathanael said to him, "Can any good thing come out of Nazareth?" Philip said to him, "Come and see." Jesus saw Nathanael coming to him, and said about him, "Behold, an Israelite indeed, in whom is no deceit!" Nathanael said to him, "How do you know me?" Jesus answered him, "Before Philip called you, when you were under the fig tree, I saw you." Nathanael answered him, "Rabbi, you are the Son of God! You are King of Israel!" Jesus answered him, "Because I told you, 'I saw you underneath the fig tree,' do you believe? You will see greater things than these!" He said to him, "Most certainly, I tell you all, hereafter you will see heaven opened, and the angels of God ascending and descending on the Son of Man." John 1:43-50

This is an incredible moment between Jesus and Nathanael. Once Jesus opened the realm of the supernatural by speaking a word of knowledge, He was able to expand on that encounter, linking it to a future promise of *greater* things and *greater* encounters. This was all made possible by a simple word of knowledge for a man sitting under a fig tree. Notice that after Nathanael responded with such humility and receptivity, Jesus expanded the word. And you can rest assured that Nathanael had that open heaven encounter. It may not be documented in the New Testament, but if Jesus said it would happen, we can assume it did.

It is possible for you and I to prophecy and speak simple words of knowledge to individuals that can totally transform their future on multiple levels and position them to receive a blessing from God, hearing from God and learning to discern His voice and even repeat what He is saying.

Once the line of communication is open between you and heaven you will hear plenty from God. As we hear what He reveals, we must learn to speak it. But be sure to only speak what you hear or see. Never over analyze it, and don't try to rustle up a meaning unless of course the Lord tells you what it means. My

personal experience is that if I try to define the prophecy or word of knowledge with my own *opinion* of what it *might* mean, I fall way short and could even derail it by narrowing their view and expectation. There are other times when I know exactly what the word means and am compelled to say so. This usually happens when the very word itself is descriptive in nature.

Understanding and embracing the prophetic potential within you will transform your world and the world around. After all the least in the kingdom is greater than John the Baptist.

"For he that is least among you, the same shall be great" Luke 9:48

25. Becoming An Encounter

Remember the story at the beginning of chapter one? Here's the first part again:

The restaurant was not too busy. I had never eaten there before, but the décor was inviting and the menu was appealing so I gave it a whirl. My waitress was very inquisitive, and after multiple questions about who I was and where I was from, I finally told her I was passing through on a speaking engagement for a local church. She looked very surprised. I'm not very pastoral looking. My head is shaved, I was wearing skinny jeans and a t-shirt, and both my arms are covered with tattoos. I didn't fit the profile of a traveling preacher.

She quickly responded, "I don't believe in God, I only believe in things I can prove." To her surprise I was totally unaffected by her statement. I matter-of-factly said something like, "that's cool." I placed my order, and all was well between us. About ten minutes later, she returned with my order. It looked good: pan-fried garlic shrimp in a bed of fresh pasta. She knew I was impressed by this presentation, especially in such a small and inconspicuous restaurant.

Before she walked away from my table I asked her "why are you leaving town?" Her face went from an ear-to-ear smile to dead cold and bug-eyed. She leaned into my table and under her breath said, "How did you know? I haven't told anybody,"

Without flinching, I said: "the God you don't believe in just told me, and He wants you to know that if you stay in this city, the very things you hope and dream for will come to pass."

Now here's the rest:

Her eyes filled with tears, and she quickly walked away, never to return to my table. She served the tables around me without even glancing in my direction. I had to ask for my check, and another waitress rung me up at the cash register.

That's probably not exactly what you expected. But I wanted to show that not all encounters with the presence of God end up with a person falling to their knees asking Jesus to come into their heart. But! You can rest assured that the waitress was dramatically affected by the moment, and, just from her reaction when I told her what I heard, I believe she went away with much to think about. God spoke to her directly from heaven, and she couldn't deny it—even if she couldn't "prove" it. Her barrier of unbelief had been penetrated.

As much as God wanted the waitress to hear from Him, He wanted me to hear from Him—and to obey Him when He asked me to speak. Obedience to His voice opens the door for Him to speak often. And the Lord loves to talk.

26. The Power Of Raw Obedience

The testimony you are about to read is a fitting and humble closing for this book. It reveals who I have become in Christ over the past few years—a far cry from my 1989 self at Disneyland.

It might sound odd, but I enjoy going to the city dump. I remember as a kid growing up in the suburbs or Orange County California, a trip to the city dump with my father was the equivalent of a trip to the countryside for a city kid. We would leave the congestion of never-ending traffic lights and head for the hills. I remember the feeling of coming over the final hill, with my dad's 1962 Ford truck full of our household trash, and looking down into the huge valley filled with mountains of humanity's garbage.

The whole scene excited me. Bulldozers scurried about, shoving the trash into piles. Earthmovers heaved dirt around. And then all the small trucks of patrons lined up in rows, unloading the heaps of trash and junk that were piled on their backs. In my mind, something good and industrious was happening. And to this day, I still get that feeling. And it takes everything within me to refrain from searching for discarded treasures

In 2013, I purchased a retired, three-bay auto mechanics shop in Anderson California, a small town next to Redding where I live. When I wasn't traveling for ministry or business, I loved to go work on the building. I spent months gutting it and had to take multiple trips to the city dump, or, as it is called today, the Waste Management Site. As I was relieving my trailer of its massive load of remodel debris, an elderly couple backed their truck alongside of me and began to pull their bags of trash out onto the ground.

I heard the Lord speak directly to me, "tell them I am healing their daughter." I kept on working, but I knew God had spoken and I found myself trying to figure out how to break the ice with these folks. They never once looked my way even though our vehicles were only five feet apart.

Being the great man of faith that I am, I shouted out to the man, "How do you like your truck?"

He looked over his shoulder at me with his furrowed brow and said, "It belongs to my daughter."

At that point, I knew I should have just said what the Lord said. God didn't say, "Ask them how they like the truck." But I also knew the situation was redeemable.

So I answered back, "Is she okay?"

The man was totally uninterested in any level of conversation, but his wife quickly responded, "She has cancer, and she is seeing her specialist right now as we speak. They are going to determine weather or

not to have more surgery." She was very warm and receptive in her tone.

I told her what the Lord told me a few minutes prior: "The Lord told me to tell you that He is going to heal her."

At this point, the husband quickly climbed into the truck and started the motor. He wanted nothing to do with the conversation. But his wife opened up to me and told me that she was a Catholic and that she has been going to her parish every day and praying for her daughter. It was such a joy and an honor to say what I said next. I told her, "The Lord has heard your prayers, and your daughter will be healed." Her face lit up as she thanked me for the kind words.

I don't know these people, and I don't know if I will ever see them again, but I have no doubts about their daughter's healing. On the other hand, I also went away mad at myself for not being perfectly obedient. A greater measure of faith could have been released had I just proclaimed the words of the Lord: "God say's he is healing your daughter." Instead, I eased my way in with small talk, which probably caused them to question the encounter and could have robbed it of its potential power. Even though the wife was a woman of faith, the husband could possibly bring up the fact that *he* mentioned their daughter *first*. I can see the possibility of the conversation being downgraded to the equivalent of psychic parlor tricks. As I drove away, not only did I rejoice in the Lord praising Him for His faithfulness, I also asked for His forgiveness for not obeying perfectly. Then I prayed for the daughter, asking that my stubbornness and reluctance not be held against her or her parents, and interceded in prayer on their behalf asking that the words that I spoke would land on soft, fruit-bearing soil.

I want to salt your tongue towards the simple acts of great faith in your day-to-day world. Listen for His voice while at a restaurant, on the job site, at the dump—everywhere. The greatest ministry opportunity you have is with whomever you find yourself standing, walking or sitting next to. In doing so the miraculous lifestyle you hope and dream of will happen right before your very eyes.

In the past four years I have been the ministering hands of countless miracles and in some cases terminal diseases completely healed. I have had the pleasure of speaking words of knowledge and prophesying to hundreds of individuals and along with that the joy and excitement of hearing later how the prophecies came true. Once the miracle realm takes hold on your life the rate of increase is rapid and the joy of knowing Jesus amplifies exponentially.

You can do this. The hands that heal are your hands. The words that comfort are your words. The heart that loves is your heart. The prophetic voice that brightens the future is your voice. It is Christ in you, the hope of glory.

A voice came out of the the cloud saying, "This is my beloved Son. Listen to Him!" Luke 9:35

Thanks for reading this book. May the Lord bless and confirm these words and embed them into your heart as you embark on the amazing journey of a new, powerful, and victorious walk with Jesus Christ, the Holy Spirit and Papa God.